FIRST EDITION 1971

COINS
of
CANADA

by
J. A. HAXBY
and
R. C. WILLEY

Copyright © 1971

WESTERN PUBLISHING COMPANY, INC.
WHITMAN COIN SUPPLY DIVISION
RACINE, WISCONSIN, U. S. A.

No. 9058-175

Printed in U.S.A.

TABLE OF CONTENTS

ACKNOWLEDGMENTS

The authors wish to express their sincere thanks and appreciation to the
following individuals for their assistance and contributions, both direct and
indirect, to this volume:

Walter D. Allan   R. H. M. Dolley   Major Fred Pridmore
R. C. Bell   J. Douglas Ferguson   Neil Shafer
George Blenker   Earl C. Grandmaison   Thomas Shingles
Fred Bowman   Leslie C. Hill   Thomas S. Shipman
K. E. Bressett   Dr. J. P. C. Kent   Holland Wallace
Major Sheldon S. Carroll   C. F. Martin
Myron Cook   Alfred E. H. Petrie

1

INTRODUCTION

THE COLONIAL COINAGES OF CANADA

The Colonial coinages of Canada began in 1670 with the French colonial 5 and 15 sols of Louis XIV. They cover a period of almost two hundred years and include approximately a thousand varieties. As a listing of all these would make the present catalog too large, only about four hundred of the most important are included here, many of them being illustrated for the first time.

Some pieces formerly listed in Canadian catalogs are now eliminated, for they were never intended for use in Canada. The Anchor money, the "Colonial" patterns of 1/50 and 1/100 of a dollar, and the "John Law" coinage of France are omitted from the present work for this reason. Anchor money was coined for Mauritius and the British West Indies. A few specimens may have reached the Atlantic colonies in the course of trade with the West Indies, but they were never officially recognized in Canada. The "Colonial" patterns were struck for circulation in Sierra Leone, where it had been planned to introduce a decimal system based on the Spanish dollar. When it was decided instead to adopt sterling, the coinage was abandoned, and only a small number of proofs exist today. The "John Law" coinage was strictly French, it being forbidden to export it even to the French colonies until after 1724.

The term "Canadian tokens" used to describe these coinages is abandoned as inaccurate, whatever the inscriptions may be on the coinages. These pieces are tokens in the sense that they were not intrinsically worth their face value and, for the most part, unofficially made. It is the belief of the authors that these colonial issues should be forever separated from the vast numbers of trade tokens struck after 1867, which were not universally accepted as money as were the colonial issues. Trade tokens were valid only in the communities where they were issued, and were often redeemable in goods or services and not in cash. The colonial coinages were acceptable within the colony of issue, even though they may have borne the name of a particular local merchant. Their validity was unrestricted within their province of issue unless too many of any one type were issued, when they would be discredited and refused, as occasionally happened.

In colonial times the basic copper coin was the halfpenny. The economy was such that farthings were too small to be of any use. The penny was a convenient double unit, and was issued in smaller quantities as a rule. The colonial coinages began because of the shortage of coin in the colonies. France endeavored to supply her colonies with coin, but her colonial policies were such as to keep trade balances always unfavorable, and coined money was therefore exported.

Great Britain at first could not supply the colonies with coin. After 1800 private individuals took matters into their own hands and issued coppers. When these became too numerous, the local governments had to step in and regulate the coinage, replacing the private issues with semi-regal or bank issues.

When the decimal system was adopted, the semi-regal and bank issues were allowed to continue in circulation, an Act of 1870 fixing their value at one cent per halfpenny and two cents for each penny. It was nearly 1890 before the colonial coppers were withdrawn from circulation and enough cents were in use.

INTRODUCTION

THE MANUFACTURE OF COINAGE DIES
The Development of the Matrix-Punch-Die System

The usual method of making coins is to place a flat metal disc (the planchet or blank) between two *dies* bearing the designs and impart the designs to the blank with a sharp blow. A die has as its top the flat or slightly convex surface that will become the field of the struck coin. The design elements (e.g., portrait), which are *cameo* (raised) on the coin are *incuse* (sunken) and face the opposite direction in the die. If the reader has difficulty grasping this concept, he should press a coin onto a piece of clay. The image left in the clay is a model of what the top of the die which struck that side of the coin looked like.

In ancient times and for many years thereafter, dies were individually hand engraved. This system was extremely laborious, and once any given die wore out, its precise design was lost for future coinages. Gradually, more complex systems arose, with the ultimate result of preserving a design for an essentially indefinite period.

The first refinement in die-making technique was to engrave the device (e.g., the portrait) in the form of a *punch*. A punch is a steel intermediate that has its design in cameo, in the same sense as on a coin. The design of the punch would then be impressed into blocks of steel, each of which would become a die. All secondary details (legends, rim beads, etc.) were hand engraved into each die, as previously. The effect of the punch-die system was to extend the life of those parts of the design borne on the punches, because each punch could make ("sink") multiple dies.

The transition to the period of modern die-making occurred in the 1600's with the introduction of a third kind of intermediate, the *matrix*. A matrix has its design in the same sense as a die; however, it is used to make ("raise") punches instead of to strike coins. The addition of the matrix step offered two advantages over the previous system. First, a design could be better preserved (a matrix can be used to raise multiple punches). Second, instead of adding the legend and rim beads at the die stage, these details could be incorporated into the matrix. With only slight modifications, the matrix-punch-die system of die making has persisted to this day.

Initiation of a New Coinage Design

In modern die-making one of the fundamental problems is how to produce matrices of new design. The most direct way, but also the most difficult, is to engrave it by hand. After the outlines are scratched on the face of a steel block, the design elements are painstakingly hand cut to the exact size they are to appear on the finished coins. Lettering and other secondary features are often engraved as individual hand punches and punched into the matrix. Only a highly skilled engraver is capable of hand engraving a matrix, and this once common practice has largely disappeared today. The Canadian issues produced by this method are the Victory 5¢ of 1943-45 and the Newfoundland commemorative dollar of 1949. Both were by Thomas Shingles, the Royal Canadian Mint's former chief engraver.

The alternative method for making a matrix of a new design is to use the "reducing machine." The machine was invented by a Frenchman, Contamin, around the beginning of the 19th century and was first used in London's Royal Mint in 1824. While initially rather crude, the reducing machine has gradually evolved into a very important part of the engravers' tools. Briefly, it functions as follows: An 8″ diameter three dimensional model of the design is produced in some hard substance such as plastic (formerly electroplated metals). A tracer at one end of a lever arm systematically scans the surface of the model. At the other end of the arm is a rapidly revolving cutter that faithfully duplicates the movements of the tracer, cutting the design on a reduced scale into a steel block. The reduction from the 8″ model to coin size is usually made in two steps. Using the 8″ model as a pattern, a steel *intermediate model* (about 3″ in diameter) is made in the machine. The intermediate model is then similarly used to make a second reduction to coin scale. The second product of the machine is almost always a punch, called the *reduction punch*. The perfected reduction punch is placed in a powerful press and its design used to sink the matrix. Any details absent from the original model are then punched into the matrix. In the Victorian period reduction punches bore only the portrait or reverse device; now only the rim denticles are lacking.

Alteration of Pre-existing Designs

The creation of a partially new design from one already used for coinage can be accomplished by a number of methods. During the Victorian and Edwardian periods, the commonest means was to re-engrave a punch or matrix bearing the old design. In some cases the change was slight, in others very pronounced. The Victorian portrait modifications are an elegant example of such a process.

In the George VI and Elizabeth series changes have been more often made by re-engraving at some point prior to the matrix stage. For example, the famous 1953 modification of the Canadian obverses was made by re-engraving the intermediate model for the reducing machine (see above section).

Dating of Coinage Dies

The dating of dies for the decimal coins has been accomplished by two methods. During the Victorian period it was common practice to employ reverse punches which had only a portion of the date (the first two or three digits). Dies sunk from such punches would then be finished by punching in, one digit at a time, the missing portion of the date. Occasionally, the date was completed at matrix stage.

The post-Victorian dies have usually been prepared from fully dated matrices. Notable exceptions, however, are the 50¢ and dollars for part of the 1940's and the early 1950's, where the date was once again completed in the dies.

Chromium Plating of Coinage Dies

During World War II, an attempt was made to increase die life. The most important advance was the development of an electrolytic process whereby a thin layer of pure chromium was deposited on the die faces. This gave the desired increase in die life and also imparted a better finish to the coins. Following limited use in 1942-44, chromium plating was adopted for all coinage dies in 1945.

This process, for all its advantages, has also led to the creation of two kinds of trivial differences between coins. First, it sometimes happens that

INTRODUCTION

tiny pieces of the plating chip away, leaving pits in the die faces. Such pits are manifested on the struck coins as tiny, irregular "dots." (e.g., the 1947 "dot" coins). Second, during the late 1940's and part of the 1950's, serviceable dies with degenerated plating were replated and put back in the presses. One danger of this was inadvertent removal of delicate design details when the dies were repolished. The 50¢ 1950 "no lines in 0" and 1955 (and other so-called) "Arnprior" dollars are doubtless traceable to this practice. Replating of dies is no longer done at the Mint.

MINTS, MINT MARKS
AND QUANTITIES OF COINS STRUCK

Prior to 1908, all decimal issues for British North America were struck in England. The matrices, punches and dies were prepared at the Royal Mint in London and, when time permitted, the coins were also struck there. As the Mint's work load increased, it was necessary to sometimes send the dies to the Heaton Mint (after 1889 called The Mint, Birmingham), where the coins were struck on contract.

With the single exception of the 1871 Prince Edward Island cent, Heaton-struck coins bear a small H mint mark. The last Heaton issue for British North America was the Canadian cent of 1907. Locations of the H are as follows: *Canada:* 1¢ 1876-90, 1907: below date; 1898, 1900: below bottom leaf; 5-50¢ 1871-1903: below bow of wreath; *Newfoundland:* 1¢ 1872-1904: below bow of wreath; 5-50¢ 1872-76: below bust; 1882: below date; $2. 1882: below date.

Late in the 19th century, the Canadians began agitating for a domestic mint with the power to coin sovereigns. Such an institution was authorized by the Ottawa Mint Act of 1901. However, construction was not begun until 1905, but was finally completed in time for commencement of coinage on 2 January 1908.

The name of the new mint was The Royal Mint, Ottawa Branch, but this was changed to The Royal Canadian Mint on 1 December 1931 when it became part of the Canadian government's Department of Finance. The Mint is now a Crown Corporation (since 1969), which reports to Parliament through the Minister of Supply and Services.

Certain of the 20th century Newfoundland coinages have been struck at the Ottawa Mint; they are designated with a C (Canada) mint mark on the reverse: 1¢ 1917-20: below bow of wreath; 1941-47: above T of CENT; 5-50¢ 1917-47: at bottom reverse below oval. In addition, Ottawa-struck English type sovereigns of 1908-18 have a raised C mint mark centered on the base of the design above the date.

Although mintage figures given in this catalog have been obtained from official sources whenever possible, those for the period 1858-1907 must for the most part be considered approximate. This is because the Royal Mint often attempted to use up all good dies, even if they bore the previous year's date. Therefore, while the reported number of coins struck in a given year may be quite correct, one cannot be certain what proportion were actually of that date. A good example of the problem is the Canadian 10 cents issue dated 1889. Research results have pointed to the scarcity of that date (reported mintage 600,000) as the result of 1888 dies having been used to strike most of the pieces.

VARIETIES AND ODDITIES

Collectors have long been interested in differences between coins not only because of denomination and date but also in patterns of changes made in the designs of individual series. There can be variations in the precise details of portraits, the style or size of lettering or date, and so on. Such items have become increasingly popular, and a study of varieties can transform an otherwise placid series into an exciting one.

Together with the rise in variety interest has come a group of terms to describe these differences. Two coins are different *types* if their designs show some *basic* difference. For example, the Elizabeth II 1953-64 vs. the 1965-obverses represent separate types. One critical distinction is the presence of a laureated bust on the former and a diademed bust on the latter. Conversely, the "broad leaves" vs. the "small leaves" Canadian 10¢ reverses of George V are of the *same* type. The designs certainly differ in fine details; however, the basic appearance was unchanged.

The above mentioned George V 10¢ examples are *major varieties,* meaning that there is an obvious and deliberate alteration without changing the basic design. Less apparent varieties are termed *minor varieties* or *variants.* When the difference was actually prepared in the dies, the resulting coins will show variations called *die varieties.* Examples of *non-die varieties* are the changes in metallic composition in the 1968 10¢ and 25¢ from part silver to nickel.

Not all coins that differ from each other are varieties. The latter designation is reserved for coins differing as a result of some deliberate action by the issuing mint. Any variations arising from such causes as deterioration of dies or malfunction of mint machinery are not true varieties. They are *freaks* or *oddities.* Another often used label is "mint error." This term, however, is usually not appropriate and its use should in most cases be avoided.

While wishing to avoid creating a work primarily for variety specialists, the authors also recognize that even non-specialists are showing increasing interest in the more noteworthy varieties. Furthermore, to list a few varieties while omitting others that are at least as important is illogical and extremely misleading. An attempt has therefore been made to include *all noteworthy varieties* known to us.

A small number of oddities and more trivial varieties have also been included. This was deemed necessary because the particular items in question have been widely publicized as important differences.

Finally, it must be emphasized that this book is only a guide, and that by inclusion of a given item the authors do not necessarily suggest that it should be part of a "complete" set. Each collector is urged to decide for himself the extent of his interest in the sub-listings.

COMMEMORATIVE ISSUES

Canada is a country with a rich history, and many of its important events or occurrences have been featured with special coinage designs.

1935 dollar — The obverse of the first Canadian dollar bore an inscription for the Silver Jubilee of King George V.

1939 dollar — A Parliament buildings reverse motif honored the Royal Visit by King George VI, Queen Elizabeth and Princesses Elizabeth and Margaret.

1949 dollar — A ship reverse marked the entry of Newfoundland into the Dominion of Canada.

INTRODUCTION

1951 5 cents—The bicentenary of the isolation and naming of the element nickel was commemorated with a nickel refinery design on the reverse.

1958 dollar—A totem pole reverse motif was employed as part of the centenary celebration of the western gold rush and the establishment of British Columbia as an English Crown colony.

1964 dollar—The 100th anniversary of the meetings that paved the way for later Confederation was marked by the issuance of a special reverse for this denomination.

1967—All of the regular denominations (1¢ to $1.) bore special reverses to honor the centenary of Confederation. A $20 gold piece was also made and sold with the commemorative sets though it has no specific commemorative legend.

1970 dollar—A prairie crocus reverse design commemorated the centenary of the entrance of Manitoba into the Dominion of Canada.

1971 dollar—The 100th anniversary of British Columbia's becoming part of the Dominion of Canada was marked with a coat of arms reverse.

CONDITIONS OF COINS

The condition of a coin describes the *amount of wear* it has sustained since it was minted. Determining the grade of condition is one of the most important skills the beginning collector must study and master. For some more expensive coins, the difference in value from one grade to the next can amount to hundreds of dollars.

Regardless of the series involved, some basic principles about grading should be borne in mind:

(a) The grade of a coin is independent of rarity; standards should not be lowered for scarcer items.

(b) Grading should also be uniform whether the coin is being bought or sold!

(c) When a coin is mutilated, corroded, stained or has some other significant flaw, it is first graded as though these defects were absent. Obviously, as serious impairment does lower the value of a coin, such impairment which is not the result of normal wear must be included separately in the description of the condition of any coin.

Usually, a given design has some key areas which have a characteristic pattern of wear for each of the circulated grades. The George V coinages, for example, are graded primarily by the head band of the King's crown. Brief statements of grading for each series are included in the listings. In general terms the various grades have the following characteristics:

Proof, Specimen or Prooflike — Not a condition; (see pages 69 and 70) this is simply a process of striking which produces a special effect on the finished coins, usually very sharp and with a mirrorlike surface.

Uncirculated (Unc., mint, mint state) — No frictional wear is present. Coins issued in mint bags often have minor surface abrasions, caused by contact with other coins. Pieces showing *full original* mint luster (bright reddish or gold for bronze or copper) are termed brilliant uncirculated (B.U.) and, particularly in the case of pre-1937 bronze issues, can command a substantial premium over toned pieces.

Extremely Fine (E.F.) — Wear is just noticeable on the highest parts of the design. The device (portrait, wreath, etc.) details are still clear and sharp.

INTRODUCTION

Very Fine (V.F.) — Device details are somewhat worn, but still clear. The highest parts of the design are clear, but not all necessarily sharp.

Fine (F.) — Wear is in clear evidence. Some details of the devices have worn away.

Very Good (V.G.) — Devices show much wear, but some of the details still remain.

Good (G.) — Many details are virtually obliterated. Outlines of the devices and all other basic parts of the design must be clear.

Fair (Fr.) — Only very scarce and rare coins are collected in this condition. The coin is worn so badly that portions of the legends or date have become indistinct.

For additional details on the grading of Canadian coins, *The Standard Grading Guide to Canadian Decimal Coins* by J. E. Charlton and R. C. Willey should be consulted.

RARITY AND VALUE

When one inquires as to the rarity of a coin, it is not really sufficient to specify merely the date and denomination. Varieties exist for several issues, and where they are particularly noteworthy, they are often widely collected as distinct entities — that is, as if they were separate dates. It is also best to specify the condition of the coin. There is always a marked difference between the rarity of earlier issues in uncirculated vs. well circulated conditions. Compare values for the various conditions of the Canadian 1911 50¢. In Very Good (well circulated) it lists at $4, but in uncirculated it jumps to $750!

Because determining rarity by the direct method of examining a large number of coins is often impractical, it is usually deduced by other means. A common practice is to compare prices. This method, while certainly a reasonable starting point, can sometimes be very misleading. For example, the Canadian 1921 50¢ in uncirculated condition lists for $6,500 while the 1870 50¢ without the designer's initials has been valued at nearly $1,000 in the same condition. Is the latter coin, then, six times commoner than the former? The mint state 1870 is in fact twice as rare as the 1921. Why the inverted price relationship? The 1870 is part of a series not widely collected by date and variety, and its rarity is much less appreciated than that of the famous 1921.

The other usual way to ascertain rarity is by comparing mintage figures. Here, too, caution is in order. First, reported figures especially for the Victorian period (see above), are not always reliable. Second, in the case of varieties the mints rarely know what proportion of a given year's issue was of a particular variety. And third, mint figures tell one nothing about the number of pieces preserved in the better conditions. Example: the mintages for the Canadian 1937 and 1938 50¢ are almost identical, yet the uncirculated valuation for the 1937 is $17.50 while that for the 1938 is $100. The 1937's were saved in quantity because they were the first date of a new series. On the other hand, most of the 1938's went into circulation.

The value of a coin is determined by the law of supply and demand. Some very scarce items change little in value from year to year simply because

INTRODUCTION

they are not widely collected, whereas commoner dates that are part of a very popular series can show great differences.

The approximate market values listed in this catalog are only indications of probable average worth. In an individual transaction a coin may sell for more or less than what is indicated here. Every attempt has been made to quote values that realistically reflect the market. These values were determined by a panel of several individuals, most of whom are in close contact with retail sales. In some instances, particularly for previously unpublished varieties, the prices are either theoretical or omitted.

LOCAL AND NATIONAL
NUMISMATIC ORGANIZATIONS

Throughout Canada and the U.S. are located many local coin clubs that include in their memberships those interested in any and all phases of numismatics. Becoming involved in such an organization offers important advantages to beginner and more experienced collector alike. One can acquire needed coins, dispose of extras, gain valuable knowledge and enjoy the good fellowship of others with like interests.

Similarly, anyone seriously interested in Canadian numismatics should join and support Canada's national numismatic organization, The Canadian Numismatic Association. Its members have access by mail to the association's impressive library and receive the Canadian Numismatic Journal, the official monthly periodical. The "Journal" provides a medium for publishing and disseminating numismatic knowledge, so important for progress in the hobby. Those interested in membership should contact:

> The Canadian Numismatic Association
> Mrs. Louise Graham (General Secretary)
> P.O. Box 313
> Willowdale, Ontario, Canada

There is also an organization for those interested in paper money:
> Canadian Paper Money Society
> Box 7 Postal Station S
> Toronto 382, Ontario, Canada

And, finally, the principal national U.S. numismatic association (the largest in the world) is:
> The American Numismatic Association
> P.O. Box 2366
> Colorado Springs, Colorado   80901
> (Membership inquiries should be directed to the
> General Secretary.)

DECIMAL COINAGE 1858 TO DATE

Although the early 19th century coinage of commerce in all the British North American colonies was ostensibly that of England, the actual coins were scarce and issues of a number of countries were used. They were primarily those of Spain, Portugal, France, Mexico and the United States. Furthermore, as outlined in other chapters, large numbers of privately issued base metal pieces circulated for pence and halfpence. The need for unified currencies was clear-cut. The ultimate result was a distinctive decimal currency for each of the colonies.

The principal leader in the Province of Canada's struggle for its own coinage was Sir Francis Hincks, Inspector General (1848-54), Prime Minister (1851-54) and later the first Minister of Finance for the Dominion of Canada. Legislation establishing the Province's decimal coinage consisted of several steps that took almost a decade. Initially there was strong British opposition.

In 1850 an act was passed which empowered the provincial government to have its own distinctive coinage struck in pounds-shillings-pence denominations. The British government disallowed the act, however, partly because it was felt that the regulation of coinage was the prerogative of the Sovereign and the use of English currency facilitated trade with the Mother Country.

In a second act, passed in 1851, the Canadians continued the fight for control of their own currency. For the first time a decimal system was suggested: public accounts were to be kept in dollars, cents and mils. The English Treasury also viewed the second act with disfavor, but did not disallow it. Instead, it was proposed that the province have its own pound and that it could be divided into decimal units if necessary.

The 1851 act paved the way for an act of 1853, which established a Canadian currency consisting of pounds-shillings-pence and dollars-cents-mils, the public accounts being kept in the latter. The striking of coins was left to the Queen's prerogative and none was issued under this act.

Finally, in 1857, the dollar alone was established as the unit of money and all accounts, public and government, were to be kept in dollars and cents. The Canadian dollar was given the same intrinsic value as the U.S. dollar; the English sovereign (pound sterling) was worth $4.86⅔. An issue of decimal coins followed in 1858-59.

1 CENT

Victoria, Province of Canada Coinage 1858-1859

The obverse, showing a very youthful Victoria with a laurel wreath in her hair, was designed and engraved by the Royal Mint's Chief Engraver, Leonard C. Wyon.

The reverse was also by Wyon and has a serpentine vine with 16 maple leaves. There are numerous slight variations involving re-cutting of some of the leaf stems or the vine stalk.

1859 date varieties. Although the Province of Canada placed its single order for cents in 1858, insufficient time forced the Royal Mint to strike the bulk of the coins in 1859. Two distinctly different 9 punches were used for dating the dies. A number of dies (at least 11) were originally dated 1858 and have the final 8 altered by overpunching with a wide, bold 9; this 9 was apparently used *only* for overdating (we cannot confirm the claims that the wide 9 occurs on a non-overdate). A second figure, used for the non-overdates, is narrow and initially rather delicate. Some narrow 9 specimens have the 9 somewhat broadened; these are thought to be from dies dated late in the issue when the narrow 9 punch had distorted from extensive use (rather than two different styles of narrow 9 punches being used). Both the delicate and broadened narrow 9's are illustrated because the latter is sometimes confused with the wide, bold 9. The so-called "narrow 9 over 8" is not a true overdate but a double-punched narrow 9 with a small piece out of the die at the lower front of the 9's. A second double-punched narrow 9 has traces of the original 9 to the left of the second figure. The latter double-punchings are considered trivial by these cataloguers; however, they are included because of current wide acceptance by collectors.

Diameter: 25.40 mm; weight: 4.536 grams; composition: .950 copper, .040 tin, .010 zinc; edge: plain.

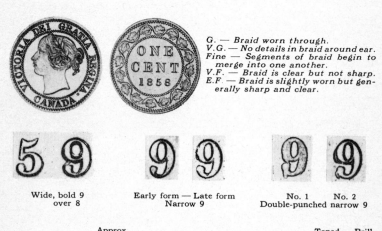

G. — *Braid worn through.*
V.G. — *No details in braid around ear.*
Fine — *Segments of braid begin to merge into one another.*
V.F. — *Braid is clear but not sharp.*
E.F. — *Braid is slightly worn but generally sharp and clear.*

Wide, bold 9 over 8	Early form — Late form Narrow 9	No. 1 No. 2 Double-punched narrow 9

Date	Approx. Minted	Good	V.G.	Fine	V.F.	E.F.	Toned Unc.	Brill. Unc.
1858	421,000	$9.00	$14.00	$20.00	$30.00	$40.00	$67.50	$140.00
1859 —								
9 over 8, wide 9		7.00	10.00	14.00	20.00	26.50	47.50	100.00
narrow 9, all forms	9,579,000	.30	.60	.85	1.25	2.50	9.00	27.00
dbl-pun. N 9, #1		17.50	25.00	32.50	42.50	55.00	85.00	125.00
dbl-pun. N 9, #2		9.00	12.50	16.50	21.00	27.50	55.00	100.00

Victoria, Dominion of Canada Coinage 1876-1901

In all, five portraits were used for the Dominion cents. Except for the first two varieties, which have the same face, the portraits differ in the facial features and in certain other respects. It is interesting that the initial portrait (P.1) was derived from one of the obverses for the Jamaica ½d. Portraits 1-3 were designed and engraved by L. C. Wyon; P.4 was probably by G. W. De Saulles. All of the varieties were created by re-engraving a previously used one. The five varieties have the following distinguishing features:

Portrait 1: Generally youthful appearance: rounded chin and prominent lips. Front lower tip of neck is pointed and nearly touches the beaded circle.

Portrait 1a: Face as P.1, but has rounded front neck tip and narrower truncation.

Portrait 2: Somewhat aged facial features: double chin and repressed upper lip.

Portrait 3: Even more aged features: double chin with a square front and depression over the eye.

Portrait 4: Smooth chin restored, but has repressed upper lip.

In addition to the portrait differences there are also several variations of lettering style, the most obvious of which occurs in association with P.3. When that portrait was used in 1890, the obverse had a normal (or nearly so) legend; however, the 1891-92 P.3 obverses *all* have a legend with more coarse style letters punched over the original.

Three major reverse varieties exist. The first (1876-82) is identical to the 1858-59 issues, except for some re-cutting of the leaf stems and vine stalk. The second has a new vine containing wider leaves with less veination. The third (1891-1901) has yet another vine containing narrow leaves with incuse veination. Each reverse was from a separate reducing machine model; the first two were by L. C. Wyon and the third is thought to be by G. W. De Saulles. There are numerous re-cuttings of the stems and stalks of the vines on the first and third reverses.

Diameter: 25.40 mm; weight: 5.670 grams; composition: .950 copper, .040 tin, .010 zinc; edge: plain.

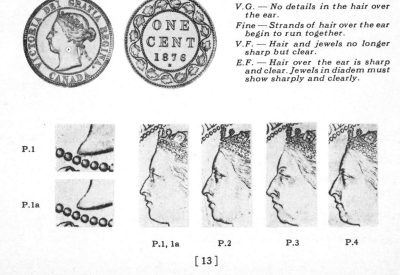

G. — *Hair over ear worn through.*

V.G. — *No details in the hair over the ear.*

Fine — *Strands of hair over the ear begin to run together.*

V.F. — *Hair and jewels no longer sharp but clear.*

E.F. — *Hair over the ear is sharp and clear. Jewels in diadem must show sharply and clearly.*

P.1

P.1a

P.1, 1a   P.2   P.3   P.4

Date	Portrait No.	Approx. Minted	Good	V.G.	Fine	V.F.	E.F.	Toned Unc.	Brill. Unc.

Provincial Leaves Reverse (1876-1882)

Date	Portrait No.	Approx. Minted	Good	V.G.	Fine	V.F.	E.F.	Toned Unc.	Brill. Unc.
1876H	1	4,000,000	$ .30	$ .60	$1.00	$1.40	$2.75	$9.00	$20.00
1881H	1, 1a	2,000,000	.50	1.00	1.50	2.50	3.75	10.00	24.00
1882H	1, 1a, 2	4,000,000	.25	.50	.85	1.25	2.00	7.50	15.00

Large leaves 1884-1891

Large date

Small date

Large Leaves Reverse (1884-1891)

Date	Portrait No.	Approx. Minted	Good	V.G.	Fine	V.F.	E.F.	Toned Unc.	Brill. Unc.
1884	1, 2	2,500,000	.40	.85	1.10	1.50	3.00	9.00	22.50
1886	1a, 2	1,500,000	.50	1.00	1.25	2.50	5.00	15.00	30.00
1887	2	1,500,000	.50	1.00	1.25	2.50	5.00	15.00	32.50
1888	2	4,000,000	.25	.50	.90	1.25	2.00	6.00	17.50
1890H	3	1,000,000	1.00	2.00	3.50	4.00	6.50	17.50	50.00
1891 lg. dt.	2, 3	} 1,452,500	1.00	2.00	3.00	4.00	6.00	16.00	50.00
s. dt.	2, 3		12.50	22.50	35.00	47.50	75.00	150.00	350.00

Small leaves 1891-1901

On the 1898 and 1900 Heaton issues the H mint mark is below the bottom leaf in the wreath.

Small Leaves Reverse (1891-1901)

Note: All *small leaves* coins, including those dated 1891, have a small date.

Date	Portrait No.	Approx. Minted	Good	V.G.	Fine	V.F.	E.F.	Toned Unc.	Brill. Unc.
1891	2, 3	Incl. above	10.00	19.00	27.50	40.00	65.00	125.00	275.00
1892	2, 3, 4	1,200,000	.60	1.25	2.00	3.00	4.50	11.00	27.50
1893	4	2,000,000	.45	.90	1.50	2.00	3.00	7.50	15.00
1894	4	1,000,000	1.50	3.25	4.75	6.50	9.75	20.00	50.00
1895	4	1,200,000	.75	1.60	2.25	3.50	5.00	12.00	25.00
1896	4	2,000,000	.40	.80	1.00	1.50	2.25	8.00	17.50
1897	4	1,500,000	.40	.80	1.00	1.50	2.25	8.00	18.00
1898H	4	1,000,000	1.00	2.00	3.00	4.50	6.75	17.50	40.00
1899	4	2,400,000	.35	.75	1.00	1.75	2.75	8.00	17.50
1900	4	1,000,000	1.25	2.75	4.00	5.00	7.50	20.00	50.00
1900H	4	2,600,000	.35	.75	1.00	1.75	2.50	10.00	17.00
1901	4	4,100,000	.25	.50	.90	1.25	2.00	7.00	17.50

Edward VII Coinage 1902-1910

A single obverse, designed and engraved by G. W. De Saulles (DES. below bust), was employed for the entire series.

The reverse was a continuation of the small leaves Victorian variety.

Diameter: 25.40 mm; weight: 5.670 grams; composition: .950 copper, .040 tin, .010 zinc; edge: plain.

G. — *Band of crown worn through.*
V.G. — *Band of the crown is worn through at the highest point.*
Fine — *Jewels in the band of crown will be blurred.*
V.F. — *Band of the crown is still clear but no longer sharp.*
E.F. — *Band of the crown slightly worn but generally sharp and clear.*

Date	Quan. Minted	Good	V.G.	Fine	V.F.	E.F.	Toned Unc.	Brill. Unc.
1902	3,000,000	$ .35	$ .75	$1.00	$1.25	$2.25	$6.00	$16.00
1903	4,000,000	.35	.75	1.00	1.25	2.25	6.00	16.00
1904	2,500,000	.40	.80	1.10	1.40	2.50	7.00	17.50
1905	2,000,000	.50	1.00	1.25	1.60	3.50	10.00	25.00
1906	4,100,000	.35	.75	1.00	1.25	2.25	5.00	15.00
1907	2,400,000	.40	.80	1.10	1.50	3.00	7.50	17.00

On the 1907 Heaton issue the mint mark is below the date.

1907H	800,000	3.00	6.00	8.50	12.00	17.50	40.00	85.00
1908	2,401,506	.35	.75	1.00	1.50	2.25	7.00	16.00
1909	3,973,339	.25	.50	.75	1.10	1.75	4.00	13.00
1910	5,146,487	.20	.45	.65	1.00	1.75	4.00	12.50

George V Large Cents 1911-1920

The original obverse, used for the 1911 issues of the 1 to 50¢, bore a legend lacking the words DEI GRATIA ("by the grace of God") or some abbreviation for them. The public complained, calling these coins "Godless," and in 1912 a modified legend containing DEI GRA: was introduced. Both varieties were derived from a portrait model of the King by Sir E. B. MacKennal (initials B.M. on truncation).

The reverse, although resembling previous designs, is completely new. The designer was W. H. J. Blakemore.

Diameter: 25.40 mm; weight: 5.670 grams; composition 1911-19: .950 copper, .040 tin, .010 zinc; 1919-20: .955 copper, .030 tin, .015 zinc; edge: plain.

Obverse 1911   Obverse 1912-1920   Reverse 1911-1920

G. — Band of crown worn through.
V.G. — Band of crown worn through at highest point.
Fine — Jewels in band of crown will be blurred.
V.F. — Band of crown is still clear but no longer sharp.
E.F. — Band of crown slightly worn but generally sharp and clear.

Date	Quan. Minted	V.G.	Fine	V.F.	E.F.	Toned Unc.	Brill. Unc.
"Godless" Obverse (1911)							
1911..........4,663,486	$ .50	$ .75	$1.25	$4.00	$12.50	$32.50
Modified Obverse Legend (1912-1920)							
1912..........5,107,642	.30	.50	.90	1.50	4.00	10.00
1913..........5,735,405	.30	.50	.90	1.50	4.00	10.00
1914..........3,405,958	.35	.75	1.25	1.75	6.00	12.00
1915..........4,932,134	.25	.40	1.00	1.25	5.00	8.50
1916..........11,022,367	.25	.35	.75	1.25	3.75	8.50
1917..........11,899,254	.25	.35	.75	1.25	3.75	8.50
1918..........12,970,798	.25	.35	.75	1.25	3.75	8.50
1919..........11,279,634	.25	.35	.75	1.25	3.75	8.50
1920..........6,762,247	.25	.35	.75	1.25	4.00	8.50

George V Small Cents 1920-1936

In order to conserve copper, the large cent was replaced in 1920 with one of smaller size, like that of the United States. The obverse bust was Mac-Kennal's familiar design and the reverse was a new design by W. H. J. Blakemore.

Diameter: 19.05 mm; weight: 3.240 grams; composition: .955 copper; .030 tin, .015 zinc; edge: plain.

V.G. — Band of the crown is worn through at the highest point.

Fine — Jewels in the band of crown will be blurred.

V.F. — Band of the crown is still clear but no longer sharp.

E.F. — Band of the crown slightly worn but generally sharp and clear.

Date	Quan. Minted	V.G.	Fine	V.F.	E.F.	Toned Unc.	Brill. Unc.
1920..........15,483,923	.15	.25	.50	1.00	4.75	8.00
1921..........7,601,627	.20	.40	.60	1.25	6.00	15.00
1922..........1,243,635	4.00	6.00	9.00	12.50	50.00	125.00
1923..........1,019,002	6.75	8.75	11.00	16.00	95.00	175.00
1924..........1,593,195	2.00	2.75	4.00	8.00	35.00	85.00
1925..........1,000,622	5.25	7.00	10.00	15.00	60.00	170.00
1926..........2,143,372	1.25	2.00	2.75	5.00	17.00	40.00
1927..........3,553,928	.60	1.00	1.50	3.00	10.00	27.50
1928..........9,144,860	.15	.25	.45	.95	4.50	10.00
1929..........12,159,840	.15	.25	.45	.95	4.50	10.00
1930..........2,538,613	.75	1.00	1.50	3.00	13.00	30.00
1931..........3,842,776	.45	.75	1.25	2.75	9.00	20.00

Date	Quan. Minted	V.G.	Fine	V.F.	E.F.	Toned Unc.	Brill. Unc.
1932 21,316,190		$.15	$.25	$.40	$.80	$4.00	$8.50
1933 12,079,310		.15	.25	.45	.80	4.00	9.00
1934 7,042,358		.15	.25	.45	.80	6.00	10.00
1935 7,526,400		.15	.25	.45	.80	5.00	9.00
1936 8,768,769		.10	.15	.25	.60	3.75	8.75

1936 dot (George VI issue — see below).

George VI Issue Struck in Name of George V

King George V died early in 1936 and was succeeded by his son Edward VIII, whose portrait was planned for introduction on 1937 coinage. Edward abdicated late in 1936, however, and his younger brother was crowned as George VI. The Royal Mint in London did not have time to prepare new Canadian George VI obverse matrices and punches for shipment to Ottawa by the beginning of 1937. This led to an emergency situation because of a pressing demand for 1, 10 and 25 cents, and in order to meet the emergency, coins were struck using George V dies dated 1936. To denote that the coins were actually struck in 1937 a small round depression was punched into each die, causing a raised dot to appear in that position on the coins. On the cent the dot is centered below the date.

Of the three denominations thus made, only the 25¢ is readily available (in circulated condition), while the two others are known only in mint state and are very rare. Obviously if all had been released they would be known in greater quantity today; therefore it seems reasonable to explain the situation in one of two ways: (a) the 1¢ and 10¢ were not struck with the dots (it has often been suggested that the depressions in these dies filled with extraneous matter or that they were never punched into the dies in the first place), or (b) they were made with dots but not issued. The first explanation is quite doubtful because (1) a former mint employee who worked in the press room in early 1937 maintains that all three denominations were struck with dots; (2) the known 10¢ specimens have a dot larger than that on the 25¢, yet the "clogging" theory would require that the 25¢ dies did not fill up while all the rest did; (3) one of the dot cents was found in the Pyx box, a container where coins taken at random from production runs are reserved for assay.

In view of the above, these authors suggest serious consideration of the possibility that the dot 1¢ and 10¢ pieces were struck but never issued (i.e., melted).

The physical specifications are as on the George V issues.

Date	Quan. Minted	Unc.
1936 raised dot below date	678,823	5 known

George VI Coinage 1937-1952

The obverses of the George VI issues are unique in that the monarch is bare-headed. The initial obverse variety has a legend containing the phrase ET IND: IMP: (for ET INDIAE IMPERATOR, meaning "and Emperor of India"). Beginning with coins dated 1948, the phrase was omitted from the King's titles, due to India having gained independence from England in the previous year. Both varieties were derived from a portrait model by T. H. Paget (H.P. under bust).

In keeping with a Government decision to modernize the designs, the simple but compelling "maple twig" design by G. Kruger-Gray (K.G. under the right leaf) was adopted for the cent.

1947 maple leaf. Some specimens of this and all the other denominations dated 1947 have a tiny maple leaf after the date, to denote that they were actually struck in 1948. In that year, while the Royal Canadian Mint was awaiting the new obverse matrices and punches bearing the modified legend (see above) from the Royal Mint in London, a pressing demand for all denominations arose. In order to meet the demand, coins were struck with 1947 obverse and reverse dies, with the leaf added to indicate the incorrect date. After the new obverse matrices and punches arrived later in the year, normal 1948 coins were put into production.

Diameter: 19.05 mm; weight: 3.240 grams; composition 1937-42: .955 copper, .030 tin, .015 zinc; 1942-52: .980 copper, .015 tin, .005 zinc; edge: plain.

Obverse
1937-1947

Obverse
1948-1952

V.G. — No detail in hair above ear.
Fine — Only slight detail in hair above ear.
V.F. — Where not worn, hair is clear but not sharp.
E.F. — Slight wear in hair over ear.

Date	Quan. Minted	V.G.	Fine	V.F.	E.F.	Toned Unc.	Brill. Unc.
ET IND: IMP: Obverse (1937-1947)							
1937........10,040,231	$ .10	$ .15	$ .25	$ .70	$1.50	$3.00
1938........18,365,608	.10	.15	.25	.70	1.50	3.00
1939........21,600,319	.10	.15	.25	.50	1.25	2.50
1940........85,740,532	.05	.10	.15	.35	1.00	2.25
1941........56,335,011	.05	.10	.15	.35	3.00	15.00
1942........76,113,708	.05	.10	.15	.35	2.75	12.50
1943........89,111,969	.05	.10	.15	.35	1.00	2.25
1944........44,131,216	.05	.10	.15	.35	1.50	5.00
1945........77,268,591	.05	.10	.15	.30	.75	1.25
1946........56,662,071	.05	.10	.15	.30	.75	1.25
1947........31,093,901	.05	.10	.15	.30	.75	1.25
1947 m. leaf...43,855,448	.05	.10	.15	.30	.75	1.50
Modified Obverse Legend (1948-1952)							
1948........25,767,779	.05	.10	.15	.35	.85	2.50
1949........33,128,933	.05	.10	.15	.20	.75	1.35
1950........60,444,992		.05	.10	.15	.50	1.00
1951........80,430,379		.05	.10	.15	.50	1.00
1952........67,631,736		.05	.10	.15	.30	.75

Elizabeth II, Laureate Bust 1953-1964

The initial obverse for the 1953 issue had a high relief, laureate portrait of the queen by Mrs. Mary Gillick (M.G. on truncation) which did not strike up well on the coins. Later in the year, the relief was lowered and the hair and shoulder detail re-engraved by Thomas Shingles, the Royal Canadian Mint's chief engraver. Two lines at the shoulder, representing a fold in the gown, are clear on the second variety but almost missing on the first. (There has been a tendency to erroneously term them "shoulder strap" and "no shoulder strap," respectively, but even on the initial portrait the ridge representing the top of the gown can be seen high above the shoulder.) The two varieties also differ in the positioning the legend relative to the rim denticles and in the styles of some of the letters.

The reverse throughout the 1953-64 period remained basically the same as that for George VI.

Diameter: 19.05 mm; weight: 3.240 grams; composition: .980 copper, .015 tin, .005 zinc; edge: plain.

No shoulder fold 1953-55

Fine — Leaves worn almost through; shoulder fold indistinct.
V.F. — Leaves considerably worn; shoulder fold must be clear.
E.F. — Laurel leaves on head somewhat worn.

Note style of letters, relation to denticles

With shoulder fold 1953-64

Date	Quan. Minted	Fine	V.F.	E.F.	Toned Unc.	Brill. Unc.
1953 no sh. fold......	} 67,806,016		$ .05	$ .10	$ .25	$ .50
shoulder fold....		$ .35	.60	1.00	6.00	15.00
1954 no fold.........	} 22,181,760		Prooflike	only:	45.00	70.00
with fold.......			.10	.20	.70	1.50
1955 no fold.........	} 56,403,193		22.50	30.00	50.00	80.00
with fold.......			.05	.10	.20	.50
1956................78,685,535				.05	.15	.30
1957................100,601,792				.05	.10	.20
1958................59,385,679				.05	.15	.20
1959................83,615,343				.05	.10	.15
1960................75,772,775				.05	.10	.15
1961................139,598,404						.10
1962................227,244,069						.10
1963................279,076,334						.05
1964................484,655,322						.05

Elizabeth II, Tiara Obverse 1965-1966

In 1965 an obverse with a new style portrait by Arnold Machin was introduced. The Queen has more mature facial features and is wearing a tiara. Two obverse varieties exist for 1965: the first has a flat field and small rim beads, while the second has a concave field (it slopes up toward the edge) and large rim beads. The second obverse was instituted because unacceptable die life was being obtained with the first. The large beads obverse, however, also had to be replaced because of a tendency for the rim detail in the dies to wear too rapidly. So, starting in 1966, the obverse has a less concave field and small rim beads. As with the 1953 issues, the 1965-66 varieties can be distinguished by the positioning of the legend relative to the rim beads.

1965 date and combinational varieties. Coupled with the two 1965 obverses in all combinations were two reverses, having trivially different 5's in the dates. The varieties of 5 have become popular, but the authors of this catalog do not consider them significant.

Sm. beads Lg. beads   Pointed 5 (at top)   Blunt 5
Detail at A of
REGINA

Date	Quan. Minted	Toned Unc.	Brill. Unc.
1965 small beads, pointed 5 . . . . (Var. 1)		$ .25	$ .50
small beads, blunt 5 . . . . (Var. 2)	304,441,082		.05
large beads, pointed 5 . . . . (Var. 3)		1.00	3.00
large beads, blunt 5 . . . . (Var. 4)			.10
1966	183,644,388		.05

Confederation Centennial 1967

All denominations for 1967 bore special reverses to commemorate the 1867 confederation of the provinces of Canada, Nova Scotia and New Brunswick to form the Dominion of Canada. The designer was Alex Colville, the device being a rock dove in flight.

1967 Confederation commemorative 345,140,645   .05

Maple Twig Reverse Resumed 1968-

Date	Quan. Minted	Brill. Unc.
1968	329,695,772	$ .05
1969	335,240,929	.05
1970		.05

5 CENTS
Victoria Coinage 1858-1901

Five different portraits of Victoria were employed for this denomination, each differing from the other in some of the facial features and in certain other respects. Except for the initial portrait, all subsequent varieties were created by re-engraving a previous design. The first and probably all later varieties were designed and engraved by L. C. Wyon. None of these was a serious attempt to accurately portray Victoria as she looked at the time.

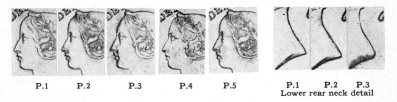

P.1   P.2   P.3   P.4   P.5   P.1   P.2   P.3
                                                    Lower rear neck detail

In some years two busts were coupled with a given date reverse. These are most easily distinguished as follows:

P.1 vs. P.2: P.1 has a convex lower rear neck profile and an incuse hairline above the eye, while P.2 has a straight lower rear neck profile and lacks the incuse hairline.

P.2 vs. P.3: P.2 has a prominent forehead, a smooth chin and a slightly rounded point at the lower right corner of the neck, while P.3 has a recessed forehead, a slight double chin and a very blunted lower right neck corner.

P.2 vs. P.5: P.2 has a prominent upper lip and a smooth chin, while P.5 has a repressed upper lip, generally "droopy" mouth and an irregular chin.

The basic reverse device consists of crossed maple boughs, tied at the bottom by a ribbon, and separated at the top by St. Edward's crown. Three major reverse varieties exist. The first (1858, 1870) has an unusually wide rim, long rim denticles and a crown with both bottom corners protruding. The second (1870-81, 1890-1901), derived from the first, has somewhat altered leaves, a narrow rim, short rim denticles and a crown on which only the left lower corner protrudes. The third design (1882-89) has an extra (22nd) maple leaf added to the lower right of the wreath of the second variety. Sub-varieties of all three reverses are known; for example, the 22nd leaf on the 1882 issue differs from and was added independently of that on the 1883-89 issues. The major and most of the minor varieties were designed and engraved by L. C. Wyon.

1858 date varieties. Most of the 1858 issue bears a small date; however, a small number of dies (4 or so) have the small date overpunched with larger, different style digits. The coins struck from each of these dies differ from each other in the relative positions of the large digits over the underlying small date. Although it has been claimed that some 1858's have a large date that is not punched over the small date, none has yet been confirmed by us.

Diameter: 15.49 mm; weight 1858: 1.162 grams; 1870-1901: 1.166 grams; composition: .925 silver, .075 copper; edge: reeded.

G. — *Braid around ear worn through.*
V.G. — *No details in braid around the ear.*
Fine — *Segments of braid begin to merge into one another.*
V.F. — *Braid is clear but not sharp.*
E.F. — *Braid is slightly worn but generally sharp and clear.*

| Wide rim, long denticles | Narrow rim, short denticles | 21 leaves 1870-81, 1890-1901 | 22nd leaf added 1882-89 (see arrow) |

Small date — Large date over small date

Date	Portrait No.	Approx. Minted	Good	V.G.	Fine	V.F.	E.F.	Unc.
Wide Rim Reverse (1858, 1870)								
1858 sm. dt.........1			$2.25	$4.50	$7.50	$12.00	$17.50	$45.00
lg. over sm. dt..1		1,500,000	32.50	50.00	75.00	100.00	150.00	285.00
plain lg. date...–			(Not yet confirmed and questionable.)					
1870.............1		2,800,000	1.75	3.50	5.00	7.50	12.50	37.50
Narrow Rim, 21-Leaf Reverse (1870-1881)								
1870.............2		Incl. above	1.75	3.50	5.00	7.50	12.50	40.00
1871.............2		1,400,000	1.90	3.75	6.50	8.00	15.00	40.00
1872H............2		2,000,000	1.00	2.25	4.00	6.25	10.00	40.00

| Plain 4, small date | Small date |
| Crosslet 4, large date | Large date |

Date	Portrait No.	Approx. Minted	Good	V.G.	Fine	V.F.	E.F.	Unc.
1874H plain 4......2			3.00	6.00	10.00	15.00	22.50	65.00
crosslet 4.....2		1,800,000	2.00	4.00	6.00	10.00	20.00	50.00
1875H small date....2			7.50	15.00	20.00	42.50	90.00	300.00
large date....2			7.50	15.00	20.00	42.50	90.00	300.00
1880H.............2, 3		3,000,000	.50	1.00	1.50	3.75	9.00	35.00
1881H.............3		1,500,000	.70	1.50	2.25	4.75	10.00	40.00

Date	Portrait No.	Approx. Minted	Good	V.G.	Fine	V.F.	E.F.	Unc.

Narrow Rim, 22-Leaf Reverse (1882-1889)

Date	Portrait No.	Approx. Minted	Good	V.G.	Fine	V.F.	E.F.	Unc.
1882H	4	1,000,000	$ .70	$1.50	$2.25	$4.75	$10.00	$42.50
1883H	5	600,000	2.25	4.50	10.00	15.00	20.00	70.00
1884	5	200,000	10.00	20.00	30.00	45.00	90.00	300.00
1885	5	1,000,000	.90	2.00	3.50	7.00	15.00	50.00

Small 6   Large 6

Date	Portrait No.	Approx. Minted	Good	V.G.	Fine	V.F.	E.F.	Unc.
1886 small 6	5	} 1,700,000	.50	1.00	2.50	5.00	10.00	37.50
large 6	5		.50	1.00	2.50	5.00	10.00	37.50
1887	5	500,000	2.00	4.25	7.50	12.50	17.50	80.00
1888	5	} 2,200,000	.60	1.25	2.50	4.50	10.00	37.50
1889	5		4.00	8.00	12.00	17.50	32.50	120.00

21-Leaf Reverse Resumed (1890-1901)

Date	Portrait No.	Approx. Minted	Good	V.G.	Fine	V.F.	E.F.	Unc.
1890H	5	1,000,000	.60	1.25	3.00	5.00	10.00	35.00
1891	5, 2	1,800,000	.50	1.00	1.50	3.25	6.50	25.00
1892	5, 2	860,000	.90	2.00	3.00	6.00	9.00	35.00
1893	2	1,700,000	.45	1.00	1.50	2.75	6.00	25.00
1894	2	500,000	2.50	5.00	7.50	10.00	17.50	40.00
1896	2	1,500,000	.50	1.10	1.75	3.25	6.00	27.50
1897	2	1,319,283	.50	1.10	1.75	3.25	6.00	27.50
1898	2	580,717	3.00	5.00	8.00	12.50	20.00	40.00
1899	2	3,000,000	.50	.85	1.50	2.25	4.25	15.00

Large date, wide 0's   Small date, narrow O's

Date	Portrait No.	Approx. Minted	Good	V.G.	Fine	V.F.	E.F.	Unc.
1900 large date	2	} 1,800,000	2.50	5.00	10.00	20.00	30.00	60.00
small date	2		.60	1.25	1.75	3.00	6.00	20.00
1901	2	2,000,000	.40	.75	1.50	3.00	4.50	20.00

Edward VII Coinage 1902-1910

A single obverse, designed and engraved by G. W. De Saulles (DES. below bust), was used for the entire reign.

With the initiation of a new series, two basic changes were to be made in the reverse designs. First, the word CANADA was to be transferred from the obverse to the reverse legend. Second, the heraldic St. Edward's crown (depressed arches), used on the English coinages throughout most of the 19th century and on the Victorian Canadian issues, was to be replaced with the Imperial State crown (raised arches). These objectives were realized on all silver denominations except the 5 cents, where a shortage of time at the Royal Mint forced a compromise. The 1902 design (London & Heaton) utilized the unaltered crown and wreath from the second variety Victorian reverse with the date and modified legend added. The presence of the outmoded St. Edward's crown caused the public to surmise that an error had been made; the 1902 coinage was consequently hoarded.

With the 1903 Heaton issue the Imperial State crown was incorporated into the 5 cent reverse. Again the wreath was derived from the second variety Victorian reverse, in this instance with slight retouching of some of the leaves. The designer and engraver for the 1902 and probably the 1903H reverses was G. W. De Saulles.

A third major reverse variety, introduced for the 1903 London issue, is from a new reducing machine model, and as such represents the first completely new reverse since 1858. The designer is presumably W. H. J. Blakemore. The maple wreath contains 22 leaves. This reverse was used every year from 1903 through the conclusion of the reign; however, in 1909-10 a major variety derived therefrom was also employed. This modification is characterized by the presence of a "†" cross *cut over* the original bow tie cross atop the crown and by sharp points along the leaf edges. The fourth variety is presumably by Blakemore, modifying his previous design.

1908 varieties. The normal reverse (bow tie cross atop the crown — see above) for 1908 has a large 8; a second variety has a "†" cross cut over the bow tie (as on the 1909-10 reverse with sharp leaf points) and a small date.

Diameter: 15.49 mm; weight: 1.166 grams; composition: .925 silver, .075 copper; edge: reeded.

St. Edward's crown 1902 only	Large H	Small H	Imperial crown, 21 leaves 1903H only

Imperial crown, 22 leaves 1903-1910	Leaves with rounded edges 1903-1910	Leaves with pointed edges 1909-1910

G. — Band of crown worn through.
V.G. — Band of the crown is worn through at the highest point.
Fine — Jewels in the band of crown will be blurred.
V.F. — Band of crown is still clear, no longer sharp.
E.F. — Band of the crown slightly worn but generally sharp and clear.

Date	Quan. Minted	Good	V.G.	Fine	V.F.	E.F.	Unc.
St. Edward's Crown Reverse (1902)							
1902	1,120,000	$ .25	$ .50	$ .90	$1.25	$2.00	$6.75
1902H lg. H...		.25	.50	.90	1.25	2.00	6.75
sm. H..	} 1,200,000	2.00	4.00	6.00	10.00	14.00	22.50
Imperial Crown, 21-Leaf Reverse (1903 Heaton)							
1903H	2,640,000	.35	.75	1.00	1.50	4.00	14.50
Rounded Leaves Reverse (1903-1910); Pointed Leaves Reverse (1909-1910)							
1903	1,000,000	.55	1.25	2.00	4.00	6.50	25.00
1904	2,400,000	.50	1.00	1.25	1.75	4.50	15.00
1905	2,600,000	.50	1.00	1.25	1.75	4.50	15.00
1906	3,100,000	.30	.60	1.00	1.50	4.00	14.00
1907	5,200,000	.25	.50	.75	1.00	2.50	13.50

"Bow tie" cross

"t" cross

Large 8   Small 8
Note shape of inner circles

Cross at top of crown

Date	Quan. Minted	Good	V.G.	Fine	V.F.	E.F.	Unc.
1908 lg. 8	} 1,220,524	$2.00	$3.00	$5.00	$7.50	$10.00	$37.50
sm. 8		1.25	2.75	4.00	6.00	9.00	32.50
1909 rd. lvs . . .	} 1,983,725	.50	1.00	2.00	2.75	4.75	15.00
pt. lvs . . .		.50	1.00	2.00	2.75	4.75	15.00
1910 rd. lvs . . .	} 5,850,325	.50	1.00	2.00	2.75	4.75	15.00
pt. lvs . . .		.20	.40	.60	1.00	2.00	7.50

George V Silver Coinage 1911-1921

Two obverse varieties exist; the first (1911) lacks the phrase DEI GRATIA or an abbreviation for it and the second (1912-21) has DEI GRA: incorporated into the legend. Both obverses were derived from a portrait model by Sir E. B. MacKennal (B.M. on truncation). See text on the 1 cent for more details.

The reverse is identical to Blakemore's rounded leaves design introduced in the Edward VII series. On 3 May 1921 the Canadian Government passed an act authorizing the substitution of a larger nickel 5 cent piece for the small silver coin. Consequently, almost the entire coinage of the silver five cents dated 1921 was melted. About 400 specimens of this date are known, most or all of which were (a) sold by the Mint in 1921 to visitors, (b) sold to those ordering year sets by mail, and (c) given to various individuals as part of 1921 specimen sets.

Diameter: 15.49 mm; weight: 1.166 grams; composition; 1911-19: .925 silver, .075 copper; 1920-21: .800 silver, .200 copper; edge: reeded.

G. — *Band of crown worn through.*
V.G. — *Band of crown worn through at highest point.*
Fine — *Jewels in band of crown will be blurred.*
V.F. — *Band of crown still clear, no longer sharp.*
E.F. — *Band of crown slightly worn but generally sharp and clear.*

1911   1912-1921

Date	Quan. Minted	V.G.	Fine	V.F.	E.F.	Unc.
"Godless" Obverse (1911)						
1911	3,692,350	.95	2.25	3.50	7.50	32.50
Modified Obverse Legend (1912-1921)						
1912	5,863,170	.40	.60	1.00	2.00	7.50
1913	5,588,048	.40	.60	1.00	2.00	8.00
1914	4,202,179	.40	.60	1.00	2.00	9.00
1915	1,172,258	1.75	3.00	6.00	10.00	35.00
1916	2,481,675	.75	1.00	2.00	3.50	10.00
1917	5,521,373	.35	.50	1.00	1.50	7.50
1918	6,052,298	.35	.50	1.00	1.50	7.50
1919	7,835,400	.35	.50	1.00	1.50	7.50
1920	10,649,851	.35	.50	1.00	1.50	7.50
1921 . . . . . . (Originally: 2,582,495)		275.00	400.00	700.00	1,100	2,200

George V Nickel Coinage 1922-1936

In order to provide a 5 cent piece of more manageable size, and "because nickel was essentially a Canadian metal" the Canadian Government introduced in 1922 a coin of pure nickel, similar in size to the United States 5 cents.

The obverse was derived from the MacKennal portrait model (initials B.M. on truncation); the reverse was designed by W. H. J. Blakemore.

1926 date varieties. Most of the 1926 issue was derived from a matrix in which the tip of the 6 is very close to the right-hand maple leaf. A second matrix (or perhaps individual die) had the 6 punched in lower, so that it was farther from the leaf. Such digit spacing and position differences are considered trivial by these catalogers; the 1926 varieties are included only because their listing in previous catalogs has led to their widespread acceptance by collectors.

Diameter: 21.21 mm; weight: 4.536 grams; composition: 1.000 nickel; edge: plain.

G. — *Band of crown worn through.*

V.G. — *Band of the crown is worn through at the highest point.*

Fine — *Jewels in the band of crown will be blurred.*

V.F. — *Band of the crown is still clear but no longer sharp.*

E.F. — *Band of the crown slightly worn but generally sharp and clear.*

Date	Quan. Minted	V.G.	Fine	V.F.	E.F.	Unc.
1922	4,794,119	$ .25	$ .50	$1.00	$4.50	$20.00
1923	2,502,279	.30	.60	2.25	6.00	32.50
1924	3,105,839	.30	.50	2.00	5.00	30.00
1925	201,921	10.00	15.00	27.50	60.00	290.00

High 6, tip near leaf

Low 6, tip far from leaf

Date	Quan. Minted	V.G.	Fine	V.F.	E.F.	Unc.
1926 high ("near") 6	938,162	1.75	3.00	6.50	17.50	100.00
low ("far") 6		17.50	27.50	60.00	90.00	350.00
1927	5,285,627	.20	.45	1.75	6.00	25.00
1928	4,577,712	.20	.45	1.75	6.00	25.00
1929	5,611,911	.20	.45	1.75	6.00	25.00
1930	3,707,673	.20	.45	1.75	6.00	25.00
1931	5,100,830	.20	.45	1.75	6.00	25.00
1932	3,198,566	.20	.45	1.75	6.50	30.00
1933	2,597,867	.20	.45	2.00	7.00	30.00
1934	3,827,303	.20	.40	1.50	6.00	26.00
1935	3,900,000	20	.40	1.50	6.00	26.00
1936	4,400,450	.20	.40	1.50	6.00	25.00

George VI, Beaver Reverse 1937-1942

Both obverses (for the round and 12-sided issues) have a bare-headed portrait of the King designed by T. H. Paget (H.P. below bust).

In keeping with a decision to modernize the new George VI reverses, the now-familiar beaver motif was chosen for the 5 cents (it was first considered for the 10 cents). The 1937 issue has a period after the date to balance the design, but after 1937 the period was omitted. The original design was by G. Kruger-Gray (K.G. left of the log).

Because nickel was needed for World War II, its use for coinage was suspended late in 1942. The substitute first used was a brass alloy commonly called "tombac." This metal quickly tarnishes to the brownish hue acquired by bronze, so the new coins were made 12-sided to avoid their confusion with the cents. Due to lack of time, the new matrices (obverse and reverse) were made without the conventional rim denticles.

Diameter 1937-42: 21.21 mm; 1942 tombac: 21.23-21.29 mm (opposite corners), 20.88-20.93 mm (opposite sides); weight: 4.536 grams; composition 1937-42: 1.000 nickel; 1942 tombac: .880 copper, .120 zinc; edge: plain.

Period after date 1937 only	No period 1938-1942

V.G. — No detail in hair above the ear.
Fine — Only slight detail in hair above the ear.
V.F. — Where not worn the hair is clear but not sharp.
E.F. — Slight wear in the hair over the ear.

Date	Quan. Minted	V.G.	Fine	V.F.	E.F.	Unc.
1937 (period after date)	4,593,263	$ .20	$ .40	$1.50	$3.00	$12.50
1938	5,661,123	.20	.40	1.75	6.00	60.00
1939	3,898,974	.20	.40	1.25	3.25	30.00
1940	13,920,197	.20	.30	.75	2.25	15.00
1941	8,681,785	.15	.30	.75	2.25	22.50
1942 round	6,847,544	.15	.30	.75	2.25	20.00
1942 12-sided	3,396,234	.90	1.10	1.25	1.50	2.50

Victory Reverse 1943-1945

This design was introduced with the aim of furthering the war effort. The obverse is as the 1942 tombac issue, except that rim denticles were added.

The torch and V on the reverse symbolize sacrifice and victory (the V also indicates the denomination, the idea coming from the U.S. Liberty 5 cents of 1883-1912). Instead of rim denticles is a dot-dash pattern forming the International code message, "We win when we work willingly." The designer was the Royal Canadian Mint's chief engraver, Thomas Shingles (T.S. at right of torch), who cut the master matrix entirely by hand — a feat few present-day engravers can accomplish.

The 1943 issue was struck in tombac; however, the alloy was replaced with chromium-plated steel in 1944-45 because the copper and zinc were needed for the war effort. The other specifications are as on the 1942 tombac issue.

Date	Quan. Minted	V.G.	Fine	V.F.	E.F.	Unc.
1943	24,760,256	$ .30	$ .50	$ .75	$1.00	$3.25
1944	11,532,784	.10	.25	.40	.50	2.00
1945	18,893,216	.10	.25	.40	.50	2.00

Beaver Reverse Resumed 1946-1952

After the conclusion of World War II the 5 cents was again struck in nickel, but the 12-sided shape had become popular and was retained. The initial obverse is identical to that of the 1943-45 issues. A second variety, introduced in 1948, incorporates the modified titles of the King (see 1 cent text). This second obverse was used for the 1948-50, 1951 commemorative, and a portion of the 1951 beaver issues. A third variety was coupled with most of the 1951 beaver and all of the 1952 issues. It is distinguished by the lower relief of its portrait and the different positioning of the legend relative to the rim denticles.

Two major reverse varieties are known. The first (1946-50) differs from the 1942 tombac issue only in having rim denticles. A second variety (1951-52) was introduced simultaneously with the change to steel composition (see below). The beaver is slightly larger and perhaps slightly lower in relief.

1947 "dot." This item is apparently the product of a deteriorated die and hence not a true die variety. Some have suggested that this was an official issue because of the fact that 25 cents and dollars (pointed 7) dated 1947 are also known with a "dot" after the date. The alternative, currently favored by most students of the decimal coins, is that the "dots" are the result of small pieces chipping out of the chromium plating of individual dies, leaving pits that would become "dots" on the struck coins. It is conceded, however, that if the latter were true it would be a remarkable coincidence. In any case the 1947 "dot" coins are probably not official because (a) the dots are irregular and of poor quality and (b) the engravers who would have officially prepared such dies are quite certain that they did not do so.

1947 maple leaf variety. This was an official issue struck in 1948, which is explained in the text for the 1 cent.

Composition 1946-50, 1951 commem.: nickel 1.000; 1951-52 beaver: steel, coated with a .0127 mm layer of nickel and plated with a .0003 mm layer of chromium. Other specifications as for 1942 tombac issue.

Small beaver 1946-1950   1947 "dot" (deteriorated die)   1947 maple leaf (official issue)

Date	Quan. Minted	V.G.	Fine	V.F.	E.F.	Unc.
Small Beaver Reverse (1946-1950)						
1946	6,952,684	$ .10	$ .30	$ .50	$ .90	$5.00
1947 normal date		.10	.30	.50	.90	5.00
"dot"	} 7,603,724		7.50	10.00	15.00	90.00
1947 maple leaf	9,595,124	.10	.25	.45	.95	6.50

Modified legend, high relief portrait 1948-1951

Note style of letters, relation to denticles

Modified Legend (1948-1952)

1948	1,810,789	.85	1.25	2.25	4.00	12.50
1949	13,037,090			.30	.50	3.50
1950	11,970,520			.30	.50	3.50

Isolation of Nickel Bicentennial 1951

As Canada is the world's largest single producer of nickel, it seemed appropriate to issue a commemorative piece upon the 200th anniversary of the isolation and naming of the element by the Swedish chemist A. F. Cronstedt. The obverse is as on the 1948-50 issues; the reverse, showing a nickel refinery, was designed by Stephen Trenka (sт monogram at lower right).

1951 commemorative	9,028,507			.25	.45	3.00

Low relief portrait 1951-1952

Note style of letters, relation to denticles

Large beaver reverse

Large Beaver Reverse (1951-1952)

1951 high relief obv.*		—	—	—		
low relief obv.	} 4,313,410			.30	.60	5.00
1952 (low relief obv.)	10,891,148			.15	.30	2.75

*Rarity not yet known.

Elizabeth II, Laureate Bust 1953-1964

The initial obverse for the 1953 issue had a high relief, laureate portrait of the Queen by Mrs. Mary Gillick (M.G. on truncation) which did not strike up well on the coins. Later in the year, the relief was lowered and the hair and shoulder detail re-engraved. The latter included sharpening two lines which represent a fold in, not a shoulder strap on, the Queen's gown. The two varieties also differ in the positioning of the legend relative to the rim denticles and the styles of some of the letters (see the 1 cent text for more details). The second portrait was not modified when the shape of the 5 cents returned to round in 1963.

Four noteworthy reverse varieties appeared during the 1953-64 period. The first is associated with the 1953 "no shoulder fold" obverse and is identical to the 1951-52 George VI beaver design. The second reverse has the design elements placed closer to the rim denticles than before. It was used for the 1953 "shoulder fold" and 1954 issues. With the return to nickel composition in 1955, the smaller beaver, last used in 1950, was restored. It continued without significant modification until 1963, when it was re-adapted to a round motif.

Diameter 1953-62: 21.23-21.29 mm (opposite corners), 20.88-20.93 mm (opposite sides); 1963-64: 21.21 mm; weight: 4.536 grams; composition 1953-54: steel, coated with a .0127 mm layer of nickel and plated with a .0003 mm layer of chromium; 1955-64: 1.000 nickel; edge: plain.

V.F. — Leaves considerably worn.
E.F. — Laurel leaves on the head somewhat worn.

No shoulder fold 1953

Note style of letters, relation to denticles

With shoulder fold 1953-1962

Large beaver 1953-1954

Design far from rim 1953

Design near rim 1953-1954

Small beaver 1955-1962

Date	Quan. Minted	V.F.	E.F.	Unc.
"No Shoulder Fold" Obverse (1953)				
1953 (no fold)......................	16,635,552	$ .15	$ .40	$2.75
"Shoulder Fold" Obverse (1953-1962)				
1953 (with fold)...................	Incl. above	.25	.75	5.00
1954..............................	6,998,662	.25	.90	4.75
Small Beaver Reverse (12-sided) (1955-1962)				
1955..............................	5,355,028	.10	.50	3.75
1956..............................	9,399,854	.10	.25	1.25
1957..............................	7,387,703	.10	.20	1.00
1958..............................	7,607,521	.10	.20	1.00
1959..............................	11,552,523	.10	.20	.50
1960..............................	37,157,433	.10	.20	.25
1961..............................	47,889,051			.20
1962..............................	46,307,305			.20

Round Coinage Resumed (1963-1964)

1963..............................	43,970,320			.20
1964..............................	78,075,068			.15

Elizabeth II Tiara Obverse 1965-1966

In 1965 an obverse with a new style portrait by Arnold Machin was introduced. The Queen has more mature facial features and is wearing a tiara.

The reverses and physical specifications during 1965-66 are as for the 1963-64 issues.

1965..............................	84,876,019			.15
1966..............................	27,678,469			.15

Confederation Centennial 1967

All denominations for 1967 bore special reverses to commemorate the 1967 confederation of the provinces of Canada, Nova Scotia and New Brunswick to form the Dominion of Canada. The 5 cents reverse device depicts a hopping rabbit. Designer: Alex Colville. The obverse and physical specifications are as for the 1965-66 issues.

Date	Quan. Minted	V.F.	E.F.	Unc.
1967 Confederation commemorative 58,884,849				$ .15

Beaver Reverse Resumed 1968-

The obverse, reverse and physical specifications are as for the issues of 1965-66.

1968. 99,253,330		.10
1969. 27,830,229		.10
1970.		.10

10 CENTS
Victoria Coinage 1858-1901

In all, six different portrait varieties of Victoria were used for this denomination. Each differs from the other in some of the facial features and in certain other respects. Except for the initial portrait, all subsequent varieties were created by re-engraving a previous design; these modifications were probably the work of the original designer, L. C. Wyon. None of them represented a serious attempt to accurately portray Victoria as she looked at the time.

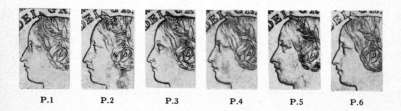

P.1   P.2   P.3   P.4   P.5   P.6

In some years two busts were coupled with a given date reverse. Such varieties are most easily distinguished as follows:

P.1 vs. P.2: P.1 has a smooth chin and a narrow truncation, extending almost the entire length of the lower neck, while P.2 has a

slightly "double" chin and a wide truncation, restricted to the
rear half of the lower neck.

P.4 vs. P.5: P.4 has a rounded forehead, smooth chin and much hairline
detail above the eye, while P.5 has a flat forehead, slightly
double chin and very little hair detail above the eye.

P.5 vs. P.6: P.5 is as described above, while P.6 has the general characteristics of P.4.

The basic reverse device consists of crossed maple boughs tied at the bottom by a ribbon. At the top is St. Edward's crown. Two major device varieties exist; the first has a wreath with 21 leaves and the second, derived from
the first, has a 22nd leaf added to the lower right. Numerous sub-varieties
of both reverses are known; for example, the 22nd leaf on the 1882 issue
differs and was added independently of that on the 1883-1901 issues. Both
of the major and most of the minor varieties were designed and engraved
by L. C. Wyon.

Diameter: 17.91 mm; weight 1858: 2.324 grams, 1870-1901, 2.333 grams; composition:
.925 silver, .075 copper; edge: plain.

21 leaves 1858-1881, 1891	22 leaves 1882-1901

G. — Braid near ear worn through.
V.G. — No details in braid around the ear.
Fine — Segments of braid begin to merge into one another.
V.F. — Braid is clear but not sharp.
E.F. — Braid is slightly worn but generally sharp and clear.

Date	Portrait No.	Approx. Minted	Good	V.G.	Fine	V.F.	E.F.	Unc.
21-Leaf Reverse (1858-1881, 1891)								
1858	1	1,250,000	$2.25	$4.50	$8.00	$14.00	$25.00	$100.00
1870	1	1,600,000	2.00	4.00	7.50	10.00	22.50	95.00
1871	1	800,000	2.50	5.00	10.00	15.00	27.50	125.00
1871H	1	1,870,000	3.50	7.50	12.50	20.00	30.00	140.00
1872H	1	1,000,000	12.00	25.00	40.00	60.00	100.00	275.00
1874H	1	} 1,600,000	2.00	4.00	7.50	10.00	22.50	85.00
1875H	1		25.00	50.00	75.00	150.00	250.00	800.00
1880H	1, 2	1,500,000	1.50	3.00	6.00	12.00	20.00	95.00
1881H	1, 2	950,000	2.00	4.00	8.00	14.00	21.00	100.00
22-Leaf Reverse (1882-1901)								
1882H	3	1,000,000	1.00	2.00	4.50	9.00	17.50	95.00
1883H	3	300,000	4.00	9.00	18.00	45.00	80.00	275.00
1884	4	150,000	12.50	27.50	55.00	95.00	200.00	650.00
1885	4, 5	400,000	2.75	5.50	12.50	27.50	60.00	150.00

Small 6 | Large knobbed 6 | Small over large 6

Date	Portrait No.	Approx. Minted	Good	V.G.	Fine	V.F.	E.F.	Unc.
1886 lg. pointed 6....5......			$2.00	$4.00	$9.00	$22.50	$40.00	$105.00
lg. knobbed 6...5......		800,000	2.00	4.00	9.00	22.50	40.00	105.00
sm. over lg. 6*..?......			—	—	—	—	—	—
small 6.........4,5....)			2.00	4.00	9.00	22.50	40.00	105.00
1887.................5.......350,000			2.25	4.75	12.50	27.50	60.00	275.00
1888.................5.....			1.00	2.00	5.00	9.50	20.00	90.00
1889.................5.....}1,100,000			75.00	150.00	250.00	400.00	650.00	2,000
1890H...............5.......450,000			2.50	5.00	9.50	20.00	50.00	175.00

Small date | Large date

1891 21 lvs, sm. dt...5......}800,000			2.75	5.50	11.00	20.00	30.00	125.00
22 lvs, lg. dt...5......			2.25	4.50	10.00	18.00	28.00	105.00
1892, 2 over 1, lg. 9*.5......}520,000			—	—	—	—	—	—
nor. dt., sm. 9..5			1.75	3.75	7.00	15.00	25.00	100.00

2 over 1, large 9 | Normal date, small 9 | Flat top 3 | Round top 3

1893 flat top 3.......5, 6....}500,000			2.25	4.50	9.50	20.00	32.50	125.00
round top 3....5, 6....			200.00	325.00	600.00	800.00	1,500	6,000
1894.................5, 6....500,000			1.50	3.00	5.00	13.00	22.50	100.00
1896.................5, 6....650,000			1.50	3.00	5.00	13.00	22.50	100.00
1898.................6......720,000			1.50	3.00	5.00	13.00	22.50	95.00

Small 9's | Large 9's

1899 small 9's.......6....}1,200,000			.80	1.75	3.00	8.00	17.50	80.00
large 9's........6.....			2.00	4.00	8.00	17.50	35.00	125.00
1900.................6.....1,100,000			.75	1.50	3.00	8.00	20.00	70.00
1901.................6.....1,200,000			.75	1.50	3.00	8.00	20.00	75.00

*Rarity not yet known.

Edward VII Coinage 1902-1910

Only a single obverse, designed and engraved by G. W. De Saulles (initials DES. below bust), was employed. The initial reverse was partially by De Saulles; the wreath was taken unaltered from Wyon's 22-leaf Victorian variety and a new legend and the Imperial State crown added. The leaves of the wreath have moderate veination, with all of the veins raised. A second variety, from a new reducing machine model, has broader leaves with extensive, incuse veination. It was designed and engraved by W. H. J. Blakemore (copying the previous design).

Diameter: 17.91 mm; weight: 2.333 grams; composition: .925 silver, .075 copper; edge: reeded.

G. — *Band of crown worn through.*
V.G. — *Band of crown worn through at highest point.*
Fine — *Jewels in band of crown will be blurred.*
V.F. — *Band of crown still clear but no longer sharp.*
E.F. — *Band of crown slightly worn but generally sharp and clear.*

Victorian leaves 1902-1909

Broad leaves 1909-1910

Date	Quan. Minted	Good	V.G.	Fine	V.F.	E.F.	Unc.
Victorian Leaves Reverse (1902-1909)							
1902............720,000		$ .80	$1.75	$3.50	$8.00	$20.00	$65.00
1902H........1,100,000		.60	1.25	2.50	5.00	10.00	35.00
1903............500,000		1.50	3.00	7.50	14.00	27.50	80.00
1903H........1,320,000		.50	1.00	2.50	6.00	12.50	55.00
1904.........1,000,000		1.25	2.50	6.50	12.50	27.50	90.00
1905.........1,000,000		.75	1.50	3.50	7.50	22.50	65.00
1906.........1,700,000		.75	1.50	3.50	7.50	22.50	65.00
1907.........2,620,000		.40	.80	2.50	5.00	12.50	60.00
1908............776,666		.60	1.25	3.00	6.00	17.50	60.00
1909.........1,697,200		.75	1.50	4.00	9.00	17.50	70.00
Broad Leaves Reverse (1909-1910)							
1909 bd. lvs..Incl. above		1.00	2.00	5.00	11.00	22.50	95.00
1910.........4,468,331		.35	.75	1.75	4.00	9.00	35.00

George V Coinage 1911-1936

Two obverse varieties exist; the first (1911) lacks the phrase DEI GRATIA or an abbreviation for it and the second (1912-36) has DEI GRA: incorporated into the legend. Both obverses were derived from a portrait model by Sir E. B. MacKennal (B.M. on truncation). See the 1 cent text for more details.

The series began with the broad leaves design introduced late in the Edward VII series. However, this was replaced in 1913 with another Blakemore design (from a new model) in which the maple leaves are distinctly smaller and have less veination.

Diameter: 17.91 mm; weight: 2.333 grams; composition 1911-19: .925 silver, .075 copper; 1920-36: .800 silver, .200 copper; edge: reeded.

G. — *Band of crown worn through.*
V.G. — *Band of crown worn through at highest point.*
Fine — *Jewels in band of crown will be blurred.*
V.F. — *Band of crown still clear but no longer sharp.*
E.F. — *Band of crown slightly worn but generally sharp and clear.*

Obverse
1911

Obverse
1912-1936

Broad leaves 1911-1913   Small leaves 1913-1936

Date	Quan. Minted	Good	V.G.	Fine	V.F.	E.F.	Unc.
Broad Leaves Reverse (1911-1913)							
1911 (no DEI GRA:)							
..........2,737,584		$2.50	$5.00	$9.50	$17.50	$35.00	$160.00
1912..........3,235,557		.30	.60	.85	2.25	6.00	42.50
1913 bd. lvs....3,613,937		10.00	17.50	55.00	125.00	250.00	725.00
Small Leaves Reverse (1913-1936)							
1913 (sm. lvs.) Incl. above		.25	.50	.85	2.25	6.00	35.00
1914..........2,549,811		.25	.50	.85	2.25	6.00	35.00
1915...........688,057		.80	1.75	4.00	12.50	30.00	175.00
1916..........4,218,114		.20	.45	.95	1.75	4.50	30.00
1917..........5,011,988		.15	.40	.90	1.75	4.50	25.00
1918..........5,133,602		.15	.25	.50	1.25	3.75	25.00
1919..........7,877,722		.15	.25	.50	1.25	3.75	25.00
1920..........6,305,345		.15	.25	.50	1.25	3.75	25.00
1921..........2,469,562		.15	.25	.75	1.50	4.50	32.50
1928..........2,458,602		.15	.25	.70	1.50	3.75	25.00
1929..........3,253,888		.15	.25	.70	1.50	3.75	25.00
1930..........1,831,043		.15	.25	.80	1.50	3.75	30.00
1931..........2,067,421		.15	.25	.70	1.50	3.75	30.00
1932..........1,154,317		.15	.25	1.00	2.00	4.50	35.00
1933...........672,368		.30	.60	1.25	3.00	6.00	40.00
1934...........409,067		.30	.60	1.25	3.00	6.00	50.00
1935...........384,056		.35	.75	2.50	6.50	12.50	125.00
1936..........2,460,871		.15	.20	.35	1.25	2.75	20.00
1936 dot (see below).							

George VI Issue Struck in Name of George V

A portion of the 1, 10 and 25 cents dated 1936 have a small raised dot on the reverse, denoting that they were actually struck in 1937 for George VI. On the 10 cents the dot is below the bow in the wreath. There is some question whether all of the dot 1 and 10 cents reported to have been struck exist today (see the 1 cent text for more details). The grading and physical specifications are as for the George V issues.

1936 raised dot below wreath......................191,237   4 known

George VI Coinage 1937-1952

The first obverse for this series has a legend containing the phrase ET IND: IMP: (for *Et Indiae Imperator,* "and Emperor of India"). Beginning with coins dated 1948 the phrase was omitted from the King's titles, as India had gained independence from England the previous year. Both varieties were derived from a portrait model by T. H. Paget (initials H.P. under bust). The obverses of this series are unique in that the monarch is bare-headed.

A Government decision was made to modernize the reverse designs for the George VI series, and the popular fishing schooner motif was selected for this denomination. At first the design was considered for the 25 cents, with the beaver design to be used for the 10 cents. Although the Government proclamation states that a "fishing schooner under sail" is shown, it is clear that the designer, Emmanuel Hahn, in fact used the famous Canadian racing yacht *Bluenose* as the source for his model. Hahn's initial H appears above the waves to the left. The small date on the 1937 issue proved to wear badly in circulation, so beginning in 1938 the date was enlarged and placed higher in the field. Some of the coins dated 1947 have a tiny maple leaf after the date. This denotes that they were actually struck in 1948. For more information see text on the 1 cent.

Diameter: 17.91 mm; weight: 2.333 grams; composition: .800 silver, .200 copper; edge: reeded.

V.G. — *No detail in hair above ear.*
Fine — *Only slight detail in hair above ear.*
V.F. — *Where not worn, hair is clear but not sharp.*
E.F. — *Slight wear in hair over ear.*

Obverse
1937-1947

Obverse
1948-1952

Small
low date
1937 only

Large
high date
1938-1952

Date	Quan. Minted	V.G.	Fine	V.F.	E.F.	Unc.
ET IND: IMP: *Obverse (1937-1947)*						
1937 (small date)	2,500,095	$1.75	$2.50	$4.00	$7.00	$17.00
1938	4,197,323	.35	.90	2.25	5.00	25.00
1939	5,501,748	.30	.75	1.25	2.50	20.00
1940	16,526,470	.25	.40	.75	1.50	7.50
1941	8,716,386	.25	.40	1.50	4.00	25.00
1942	10,214,011	.20	.30	.75	1.25	15.00
1943	21,143,229	.20	.30	.75	1.25	7.50
1944	9,383,582	.20	.30	.75	1.25	7.50
1945	10,979,570	.20	.25	.50	.90	6.00
1946	6,300,066	.20	.30	.60	1.50	10.00
1947	4,431,926	.25	.50	1.25	3.00	15.00
1947 maple leaf	9,638,793	.20	.30	.60	.80	7.00

DECIMAL COINAGE

10 Cents

Date	Quan. Minted	V.G.	Fine	V.F.	E.F.	Unc.
Modified Obverse Legend (1948-1952)						
1948	422,741	$3.25	$6.00	$8.75	$15.00	$30.00
1949	11,336,172	.20	.25	.30	.75	3.50
1950	17,823,075	.20	.25	.30	.60	3.50
1951	15,079,265	.20	.25	.30	.60	3.50
1952	10,474,455	.20	.25	.30	.60	3.50

Elizabeth II, Laureate Bust 1953-1964

The initial obverse for the 1953 issue had a high relief, laureate portrait of the Queen by Mrs. Mary Gillick (M.G. on truncation) which did not strike up well on the coins. Later in the year, the relief was lowered and the hair and shoulder detail re-engraved. The latter included sharpening two lines which represented a fold in the Queen's gown. The two varieties also differ in the positioning of the legend relative to the rim denticles and the styles of some of the letters. See text on the 1 cent for more details.

The reverse used during this period remained basically the same as that introduced in the previous series.

Diameter: 17.91 mm; weight: 2.333 grams; composition: .800 silver, .200 copper; edge: reeded.

No shoulder fold 1953

Note style of letters, relation to denticles

Fine — Leaves worn almost through; shoulder straps indistinct.
V.F. — Leaves worn considerably; shoulder straps must be clear.
E.F. — Laurel leaves on head somewhat worn.

With shoulder fold 1953-1964

"No Shoulder Fold" Obverse (1953)

1953 (no fold)	17,706,395	.20	.25	.50	3.00

"Shoulder Fold" Obverse (1953-1964)

1953 (with fold)	Incl. above	.25	.35	.95	5.50
1954	4,493,150	.30	.75	1.00	5.50
1955	12,237,294	.20	.25	.50	2.00
1956 normal	16,732,844	.15	.20	.40	1.00
"dot"		1.00	1.25	1.75	3.00
1957	16,110,229		.15	.25	.50
1958	10,621,236		.20	.30	.75
1959	19,691,433		.15	.20	.35
1960	45,446,835			.15	.25
1961	26,850,859			.15	.20
1962	41,864,335			.15	.20
1963	41,916,208			.15	.20
1964	49,518,549			.15	.20

Elizabeth II, Tiara Obverse 1965-1966

In 1965 an obverse with a new style portrait by Arnold Machin was introduced. The Queen has more mature facial features and is wearing a tiara. The reverse and physical specifications for the 1965-66 period remain as before.

Date	Quan. Minted	E.F.	Unc.
1965	56,965,392	$ .15	$ .20
1966	34,330,199	.15	.20

Confederation Centennial 1967

All denominations for 1967 bore special reverses to commemorate the 1867 confederation of the provinces of Canada, Nova Scotia and New Brunswick to form the Dominion of Canada. The design for this denomination, by Alex Colville, shows a mackerel. During the issue, the alloy was changed to .500 silver, .500 copper. The alloy varieties are not distinguishable, so only a single catalog value is given below.

	Quan. Minted	E.F.	Unc.
1967 .800 silver	32,309,135 ⎫		
.500 silver	30,689,080 ⎭	.15	.20

Schooner Reverse Resumed 1968-

Two major reverse varieties have appeared since the 1968 resumption of the fishing schooner design. The first is as the previous issue; the second, by Myron Cook (but still bearing Emmanuel Hahn's initial H), has the size of the device reduced and a smaller date placed lower in the field.

1968 varieties. The earlier portion of the 1968 issue was in silver. Later, the composition was changed to nickel. The nickel specimens are slightly darker in color and are attracted to a magnet. Due to lack of time, the Royal Canadian Mint made arrangements with the United States Mint at Philadelphia to strike many of the nickel 10 cents for 1968. The Ottawa and Philadelphia strikings differ only in the number of reeds on the edge and shape of the slots between them.

Diameter: 17.91 mm; weight: 2.333 grams (silver), 2.074 grams (nickel); composition 1968: .500 silver, .500 copper; 1968-   : 1.000 nickel; edge: reeded.

Large schooner, large
high date 1968-1969

Small schooner, small
low date 1969-

Date	Quan. Minted	E.F.	Unc.

Large Schooner Reverse (1968-69)

1968 .500 silver	70,460,000		$ .20
nickel, Ottawa	87,412,930		.15
nickel, Philadelphia	85,170,000		.15
1969*	Incl. below		—

*Rarity not yet known.

Small Schooner Reverse (1969-   )

1969	55,833,929		.15
1970			.15

20 CENTS
Victoria Issue 1858

The English shilling being valued at slightly over 24 cents and the Halifax currency shilling valued at 20 cents (there was no actual coin in the latter instance), the Province of Canada decided to issue a 20 cent instead of a 25 cent coin.

This move proved unpopular because of the ease of confusion of the coin with U.S. and later Canadian 25 cent pieces. Consequently, the 20 cents was never again issued for circulation after 1858.

In 1870, when the Dominion of Canada issued its first coins, the 25 cent piece was selected and by a proclamation dated 9 September, 1870, the old 20 cent pieces were withdrawn. Over half the issue was returned to the Royal Mint at various times between 1885 and 1906, melted and the silver re-coined into 25 cent pieces.

Both sides of the coin were designed and engraved by L. C. Wyon. The reverse device shows the familiar crossed boughs of maple.

Diameter: 20.75 mm; weight: 4.648 grams; composition: .925 silver, .075 copper; edge: reeded.

G. — *Braid around ear worn through.*
V.G. — *No details in braid around the ear.*
Fine — *Segments of braid begin to merge into one another.*
V.F. — *Braid is clear but not sharp.*
E.F. — *Braid is slightly worn but generally sharp and clear.*

Date	Quan. Minted	Good	V.G.	Fine	V.F.	E.F.	Unc.
1858	750,000	$17.50	$32.50	$45.00	$70.00	$90.00	$275.00

25 CENTS
Victoria Coinage 1870-1901

A total of five minor varieties of the Queen's portrait was used for this denomination, each differing in some of the facial features and in certain other respects. Each successive variety after the initial one was created by re-engraving one of those used previously. The initial and probably all later portraits were designed and engraved by L. C. Wyon; only on the final variety was he probably attempting to portray Victoria as she appeared in real life.

P.1

P.2

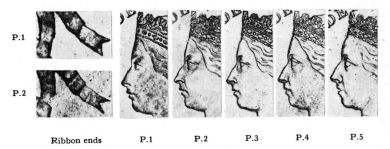

Ribbon ends   P.1   P.2   P.3   P.4   P.5

In some instances two portraits are coupled with a given date reverse. Such portraits are most easily differentiated as follows:

P.1 vs. P.2: The ribbon end extending toward the rear has a relatively constant width on P.1 but gradually narrows on P.2.

P.4 vs. P.5: The P.5 face has much more aged features and a larger nose.

The reverse device shows crossed boughs of maple, tied at the bottom with a ribbon and separated at the top by St. Edward's crown. Although there were several modifications of the design, the most noteworthy came in 1886. This second design, derived from the first, has longer cut ends to the maple boughs, slight re-cutting of other portions of the wreath and the design elements generally closer to the rim denticles. Both of these reverses were by L. C. Wyon.

Diameter: 23.62 mm; weight: 5.810 grams; composition: .925 silver, .075 copper; edge: reeded.

G. — *Hair over ear worn through.*
V.G. — *No details in the hair over the ear and the jewels in the diadem are partly worn away.*
Fine — *Strands of the hair over the ear begin to merge together and jewels slightly blurred.*
V.F. — *Hair and the jewels clear but not sharp.*
E.F. — *Hair over the ear and jewels of the diadem slightly worn, but generally sharp and clear.*

Short bough
ends 1870-1886

Long bough
ends 1886-1901

Short Bough Ends Reverse (1870-1886)

Date	Portrait No.	Approx. Minted	Good	V.G.	Fine	V.F.	E.F.	Unc.
1870	1	900,000	$2.00	$4.00	$9.00	$15.00	$27.50	$100.00
1871	1, 2	400,000	3.00	6.50	13.00	20.00	37.50	175.00
1871H	1, 2	748,000	2.75	6.00	12.50	18.50	30.00	110.00
1872H	1, 2	2,240,000	.50	1.00	2.25	6.00	15.00	100.00
1874H	2	} 2,600,000	.50	1.00	2.25	6.00	15.00	105.00
1875H	2		35.00	75.00	150.00	325.00	500.00	1,250

Wide 0 Narrow 0

1880H narrow 0	2	} 400,000	3.50	8.00	12.50	20.00	40.00	190.00
wide 0	2		6.00	12.50	32.50	70.00	135.00	325.00
1881H	2	820,000	2.00	4.00	8.00	16.00	35.00	125.00
1882H	3	600,000	2.50	5.00	10.00	20.00	40.00	135.00
1883H	4	960,000	1.00	2.00	4.00	8.00	25.00	110.00
1885	2	192,000	6.00	12.50	20.00	50.00	125.00	400.00
1886 (short b. ends)	4, 5	540,000	2.00	4.00	8.00	16.00	35.00	120.00

Long Bough Ends Reverse (1886-1901)

1886 (long b. ends)	5	Incl. above	2.00	4.00	8.00	16.00	35.00	120.00
1887	5	400,000	7.00	15.00	22.50	45.00	90.00	350.00
1888	5	400,000	2.00	4.00	8.00	16.00	30.00	115.00
1889	5	66,324	7.50	16.00	30.00	50.00	125.00	675.00
1890H	5	200,000	2.00	4.00	9.00	17.50	40.00	160.00
1891	5	120,000	3.50	7.50	15.00	30.00	75.00	250.00
1892	5	510,000	1.25	3.00	5.00	10.00	35.00	135.00
1893	5	100,000	4.00	9.00	17.50	35.00	70.00	220.00
1894	5	220,000	2.25	4.50	9.00	14.00	25.00	110.00
1899	5	415,580	.80	1.75	4.00	9.00	17.50	100.00
1900	5	1,320,000	.50	1.00	2.25	4.50	14.00	70.00
1901	5	640,000	.50	1.00	2.25	5.00	15.00	75.00

Edward VII Coinage 1902-1910

A single obverse, designed and engraved by **G. W. De Saulles** (DES. below bust), was used for the entire series.

For the first reverse De Saulles used the almost unaltered wreath from the second Victorian reverse and coupled it with the Imperial State crown

G. — *Band of crown worn through.*

V.G.— Band of the crown is worn through at the highest point.

Fine — Jewels in the band of crown will be blurred.

V.F. — Band of the crown is still clear but no longer sharp.

E.F. — Band of the crown slightly worn but generally sharp and clear.

Small crown
1902-1905

Large crown
1906-1910

and a new legend. A major modification, presumably by W. H. J. Blakemore, appeared in 1906. It has a larger crown and many of the leaves are re-engraved. The issues of 1908-10 have thickened stems.

Diameter: 23.62 mm; weight: 5.810 grams; composition: .925 silver, .075 copper; edge: reeded.

Date	Quan. Minted	Good	V.G.	Fine	V.F.	E.F.	Unc.
Small Crown Reverse (1902-1905)							
1902............464,000		$ .70	$1.50	$4.00	$9.00	$20.00	$70.00
1902H.........800,000		.60	1.25	3.00	7.50	15.00	45.00
1903............846,000		.60	1.25	3.00	9.00	30.00	100.00
1904............400,000		1.75	3.50	7.00	17.50	42.50	250.00
1905............800,000		.50	1.00	3.00	8.00	27.50	125.00
Large Crown Reverse (1906-1910)							
1906.........1,237,843		.50	1.00	3.00	7.50	25.00	100.00
1907.........2,088,000		.50	1.00	3.00	7.00	25.00	100.00
1908............495,016		.75	1.50	4.00	9.00	27.50	100.00
1909.........1,335,929		.60	1.25	3.00	6.00	32.50	125.00
1910.........3,577,569		.50	1.00	2.25	5.00	15.00	65.00

George V Coinage 1911-1936

As in the case of all other Canadian denominations, the 1911 legend did not include the phrase DEI GRATIA ("by the grace of God"). Public objection to this break with tradition resulted in the addition of the abbreviation DEI GRA: the following year. Both varieties were based on the design of Sir E. B. MacKennal, whose initials B.M. appear on the truncation of the bust. The reverse is identical to that for 1908-10.

Diameter: 23.62 mm; weight: 5.810 grams; composition 1911-19: .925 silver, .075 copper; 1920-36: .800 silver, .200 copper; edge: reeded.

Obverse 1911   Obverse 1912-1936   Reverse 1911-1936

G. — *Band of crown worn through.*
V.G. — *Band of crown worn through at highest point.*
Fine — *Jewels in band of crown will be blurred. (CAN of CANADA worn but read-able on 1936 dot.)*
V.F. — *Band of crown is still clear but no longer sharp.*
E.F. — *Band of crown slightly worn but generally sharp and clear.*

"Godless" Obverse (1911)

1911..........1,721,341	2.75	6.00	12.50	35.00	85.00	250.00

Date	Quan. Minted	Good	V.G.	Fine	V.F.	E.F.	Unc.
Modified Obverse Legend (1912-1936)							
1912	2,544,199	$ .40	$ .75	$1.75	$4.50	$12.50	$60.00
1913	2,213,595	.40	.75	1.75	4.50	12.50	60.00
1914	1,215,397	.50	1.00	2.00	6.00	15.00	80.00
1915	242,382	1.20	2.50	7.50	30.00	85.00	350.00
1916	1,462,566	.50	1.00	2.00	5.00	11.00	50.00
1917	3,365,644	.40	.75	1.50	3.00	7.50	40.00
1918	4,175,649	.40	.75	1.50	3.00	7.50	40.00
1919	5,852,262	.40	.75	1.50	3.00	7.50	40.00
1920	1,975,278	.40	.75	1.50	3.50	9.00	50.00
1921	597,337	1.40	3.00	7.50	20.00	50.00	250.00
1927	468,096	2.75	6.00	10.00	35.00	80.00	275.00
1928	2,114,178	.35	.65	1.25	3.00	6.00	40.00
1929	2,690,562	.35	.65	1.25	3.00	6.00	40.00
1930	968,748	.45	.90	1.75	3.50	9.00	70.00
1931	537,815	.50	1.00	2.50	5.50	15.00	100.00
1932	537,994	.50	1.00	2.50	5.50	11.00	85.00
1933	421,282	.60	1.25	2.75	6.00	12.50	70.00
1934	384,350	.50	1.00	2.50	6.00	15.00	90.00
1935	537,772	.50	1.00	2.50	5.00	10.00	90.00
1936	972,094	.40	.75	1.75	4.00	9.00	32.50

1936 dot (George VI issue — see below)

George VI Issue, Struck in Name of George V

A portion of the 1, 10 and 25 cents dated 1936 have a small raised dot on the reverse, denoting that they were actually struck in 1937 for George VI. On the 25 cents the dot is below the ribbon of the wreath. See text on the 1 cent for more details.

This issue seems to be particularly liable to "ghosting," thus the CAN of CANADA often will be much weaker than the rest of the legend. Nevertheless, the entire CANADA must still be readable for any specimen to grade at least V. Good. Otherwise, the grading and physical specifications are exactly as for the regular George V issues.

1936 raised dot under wreath	153,685	2.50	6.00	12.50	27.50	55.00	275.00

George VI Coinage 1937-1952

Three obverse varieties are known for this series. The first two have in common a high relief bust of the King by T. H. Paget (H.P. below); the second variety has the ET IND: IMP: omitted from the legend (see the 1 cent text). The third has a low relief modification of the original portrait. The latter variety, the work of Thomas Shingles, was made to improve the overall appearance and the clarity with which the design could be struck up. In addition to the relief of the portraits, the second and third varieties can be differentiated by the position of the legend relative to the rim denticles and by the style of some of the letters.

In keeping with a Government decision to modernize the reverse designs the caribou motif was selected for the 25 cents. At one time the fishing schooner was considered for this denomination. The designer was Emmanuel Hahn (H under caribou's neck).

1947 "dot." This item is apparently the product of a deteriorated die (see pg. 28 for more details).

1947 maple leaf variety. This is an official issue struck in 1948. See text on the 1 cent for details.

Diameter: 23.62 mm; weight: 5.810 grams; composition: .800 silver, .200 copper; edge: reeded.

V.G. — *No detail in hair above the ear.*
Fine — *Only slight detail in hair above the ear.*
V.F. — *Where not worn hair is clear but not sharp.*
E.F. — *Slight wear in the hair over the ear.*

Date	Quan. Minted	V.G.	Fine	V.F.	E.F.	Unc.
ET IND: IMP: *Obverse (1937-1947)*						
1937	2,689,813	$ .75	$1.25	$2.25	$3.75	$12.50
1938	3,149,245	.75	1.25	2.25	4.00	25.00
1939	3,532,495	.70	1.25	2.25	3.75	12.50
1940	9,583,650	.65	.95	1.25	2.00	9.00
1941	6,654,672	.65	.95	1.25	2.00	9.00
1942	6,935,871	.65	.95	1.25	2.00	9.00
1943	13,559,575	.50	.75	1.00	1.75	7.00
1944	7,216,237	.50	.75	1.00	1.75	7.50
1945	5,296,495	.50	.75	1.00	1.50	7.00
1946	2,210,810	.55	.80	1.50	2.75	22.50
1947 normal date	1,524,544	.55	.85	2.00	5.00	40.00
"dot"		6.00	9.50	12.50	20.00	125.00
1947 maple leaf	4,393,938	.50	.75	1.00	1.75	7.50

"dot" after date
(deteriorated die)

1947 maple leaf
(official issue)

High relief   Low relief

Note style of letters, relation to denticles

High relief   Low relief
1948-1952   1951-1952

Date	Quan. Minted	V.G.	Fine	V.F.	E.F.	Unc.
Modified Legend, High Relief Bust (1948-1952); Low Relief Bust (1951-1952)						
1948................2,564,424		$ .55	$ .90	$1.75	$3.50	$15.00
1949................7,988,830		.40	.50	.75	1.00	4.50
1950................9,673,335		.35	.50	.65	1.00	4.50
1951 high relief bust.... }8,290,719		.35	.40	.60	.90	4.00
low relief bust....		.35	.40	.60	.90	4.00
1952 high relief bust.... }8,859,642		.35	.40	.60	.90	4.00
low relief bust....		.35	.40	.60	.90	4.00

Elizabeth II, Laureate Bust 1953-1964

The initial obverse for the 1953 issue had a high relief, laureate portrait of the Queen by Mrs. Mary Gillick (M.G. on truncation) which did not strike up well on the coins. Later in the year, the rim width and coin diameter were increased, the obverse relief lowered and the hair and shoulder detail re-engraved. The latter included sharpening two lines which represented a fold in, not a shoulder strap on, the Queen's gown. The two varieties also differ in the positioning of the legend relative to the rim denticles and the styles of some of the letters.

The reverse coupled with the "no shoulder fold" obverse in 1953 is exactly as that for the George VI issues. Together with the obverse change, however, came a new reverse with a smaller date, wider rim and modified caribou (note the change in the contour of the lower neck). After 1953, the reverse design was not significantly altered until 1967.

Diameter 1953 large date: 23.62 mm; 1953 small date to 1964: 23.88 mm; weight: 5.810 grams; composition: .800 silver, .200 copper; edge: reeded.

No shoulder fold, high relief,   Large date, narrow rim 1953
narrow rim 1953

With shoulder fold, low relief, wide rim 1953-1964   Small date, wide rim, modified caribou 1953-1964

Fine — *Leaves worn almost through; shoulder straps indistinct.*
V.F. — *Leaves considerably worn; shoulder straps must be clear.*
E.F. — *Laurel leaves on the head somewhat worn.*

Date	Quan. Minted	Fine	V.F.	E.F.	Unc.
Large Date, No Shoulder Fold (1953)					
1953 lg. date................10,456,769		$ .40	$ .50	$ .75	$5.00
Small Date, With Shoulder Fold (1953-1964)					
1953 sm. date...............Incl. above		.40	.50	.75	4.00
1954........................2,318,891		.45	.75	1.00	12.00
1955........................9,552,505		.40	.50	.75	4.25
1956.......................11,269,353			.40	.75	2.25
1957.......................12,770,190				.60	1.75
1958........................9,336,910				.60	1.75
1959.......................13,503,461				.40	.75
1960.......................22,835,327				.35	.45
1961.......................18,164,368				.35	.50
1962.......................29,559,266				.35	.45
1963.......................21,180,652				.35	.45
1964.......................36,479,343				.35	.45

Elizabeth II, Tiara Obverse 1965-1966

In 1965 an obverse with a new style portrait by Arnold Machin was introduced. The Queen has more mature facial features and is wearing a tiara. The reverse was continued as before, and physical specifications are as on the previous issues.

Date	Quan. Minted	E.F.	Unc.
1965...44,708,869		.35	.45
1966...25,388,892		.35	.45

Confederation Centennial 1967

All denominations for 1967 bore special reverses to commemorate the 1867 confederation of the provinces of Canada, Nova Scotia and New Brunswick to form the Dominion of Canada. The design for this denomination, by Alex Colville, shows a bobcat as its device. During 1967 the alloy was changed to .500 silver, .500 copper.

Date	Quan. Minted	E.F.	Unc.
1967 .800 silver..............................	48,855,500	$ .35	$ .50
.500 silver..............................			

Caribou Reverse Resumed 1968-

During 1968, the composition was changed to pure nickel. The nickel specimens are slightly darker in color and are attracted to a magnet.

Diameter: 23.88 mm; weight: 5.810 grams (silver), 5.054 grams (nickel); composition 1968: .500 silver, .500 copper; 1968- 1.000 nickel.

1968 .500 silver.............................	71,464,000	.35	.45
pure nickel.............................	88,686,931		.35
1969..	133,037,929		.35
1970..			.35

50 CENTS
Victoria Coinage 1870-1901

In all, four portraits were used for this denomination. Except for the first two varieties, which have the same face, the portraits differ in the facial features as well as certain other respects. Each successive variety after the first was created by re-engraving an earlier one. The first and probably all later portraits were designed and engraved by L. C. Wyon; only on the final

P.1   P.2   P.1, 2   P.3   P.4
Crown and truncation details

one or two varieties could he have been attempting to portray Victoria as she appeared at the time. In some instances two portraits were coupled with a given date reverse. These are most easily differentiated as follows:

P.1 vs. P.2: P.1 has no initials on the truncation, a blank space immediately behind the front cross in the crown and a break in the left-hand ribbon end; while P.2 has L.C.W. on the truncation, a shamrock behind the front cross in the crown and no breaks in the ribbon ends.

P.3 vs. P.4: P.3 has a rounded chin front, and the lower front corner of the crown is in front of the forehead; while P.4 has a flat chin front and the lower front corner of the crown even with the forehead.

The reverse device consists of crossed maple boughs, tied at the bottom by a ribbon and separated at the top by St. Edward's crown. Although there were several slight modifications, the most noteworthy came in 1871. The second design (1871-1901), derived from the first, has parts of both the crown and the wreath re-engraved (see example in illustrations). Both reverse varieties were by L. C. Wyon.

Diameter: 29.72 mm; weight: 11.620 grams; composition: .925 silver, .075 copper; edge: reeded.

G. — Hair over ear worn through.
V.G. — No details in hair over ear; jewels in diadem partly worn away.
Fine — Strands of hair over ear begin to merge together; jewels slightly blurred.
V.F. — Hair and jewels clear but not sharp.
E.F. — Hair over ear and jewels of diadem slightly worn, but generally sharp and clear.

First reverse   Second reverse
Note recut leaf tips, veins

Date	Portrait No.	Approx. Minted	Good	V.G.	Fine	V.F.	E.F.	Unc.
First Reverse Design (1870)								
1870 no L.C.W. *1*	} 450,000		$4.00	$9.00	$17.50	$35.00	$90.00	$325.00
1870 L.C.W. on obv. . . *2*			35.00	75.00	125.00	250.00	500.00	1,000.00
Modified Reverse Design (1871-1901)								
1871. . . . .*2*	200,000		5.00	10.00	25.00	45.00	100.00	375.00
1871H. *2*	45,000		10.00	20.00	30.00	75.00	150.00	550.00

Normal 2   Short base 2   Specimens of the 1872H issue often have part or all of the reverse legend repunched.

Date	Portrait No.	Approx. Minted	Good	V.G.	Fine	V.F.	E.F.	Unc.
1872H normal 2 . . . . . 2	}	80,000	$3.50	$7.50	$17.50	$35.00	$80.00	$325.00
short base 2 . . . 2			3.50	7.50	17.50	35.00	80.00	325.00
1881H 3		150,000	4.00	9.00	17.50	40.00	90.00	400.00
1888 3		60,000	15.00	30.00	60.00	90.00	200.00	700.00
1890H 3, 4		20,000	60.00	125.00	325.00	650.00	1,250	3,900
1892 4		151,000	3.75	8.00	17.50	35.00	80.00	400.00
1894 4		29,036	15.00	30.00	80.00	200.00	500.00	1,500
1898 4		100,000	3.75	8.00	17.50	32.50	80.00	375.00
1899 4		50,000	7.00	15.00	30.00	70.00	150.00	700.00
1900 4		118,000	2.25	5.00	12.50	27.50	60.00	325.00
1901 4		80,000	2.50	5.50	15.00	30.00	60.00	325.00

Edward VII Coinage 1902-1910

A single obverse, designed and engraved by G. W. De Saulles (DES. below bust), was used for the entire series.

For the initial reverse variety (1902-10) De Saulles utilized the unmodified wreath from the later Victorian reverse with a new legend and the Imperial State crown. A modification of the first variety (probably by W. H. J. Blakemore) appeared in 1910; several leaves and the cross atop the crown differ. The most noticeable change is in the two leaves at the far right opposite CANADA. On the first variety the leaves have long, pointed corners, whereas they are much shorter on the second.

Diameter: 29.72 mm; weight: 11.620 grams; composition: .925 silver, .075 copper; edge: reeded.

G. — *Band of crown worn through.*
V.G. — *Band of crown worn through at highest point.*
Fine — *Jewels in band of crown will be blurred.*
V.F. — *Band of crown still clear but no longer sharp.*
E.F. — *Band of crown slightly worn but generally sharp and clear.*

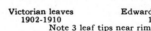

Victorian leaves   Edwardian leaves
1902-1910   1910
Note 3 leaf tips near rim

Date	Quan. Minted	Good	V.G.	Fine	V.F.	E.F.	Unc.
Victorian Leaves Reverse (1902-1910)							
1902............120,000		$2.25	$5.00	$10.00	$20.00	$40.00	$225.00
1903H..........140,000		2.25	5.00	12.50	30.00	60.00	300.00
1904............60,000		10.00	20.00	40.00	80.00	210.00	700.00
1905............40,000		6.00	12.50	25.00	60.00	140.00	600.00
1906............350,000		1.10	2.50	6.00	20.00	45.00	250.00
1907............300,000		1.10	2.50	6.00	20.00	45.00	250.00
1908............128,119		1.25	3.00	9.00	25.00	50.00	325.00
1909............203,118		1.10	2.50	6.00	20.00	50.00	200.00
1910 (Vict. lvs)..649,521		3.00	6.00	12.50	25.00	75.00	300.00
Edwardian Leaves Reverse (1910)							
1910 (Edw. lvs.)							
........Incl. above		2.00	4.00	8.00	16.00	45.00	235.00

George V Coinage 1911-1936

Two obverse varieties exist; the first (1911) lacks the phrase DEI GRATIA or an abbreviation for it and the second (1912-36) has DEI GRA: incorporated into the legend. Both obverses were derived from a portrait model by Sir E. B. MacKennal (B.M. on truncation). See the 1 cent text for more details. The reverse is identical to the Edwardian leaves variety, introduced in the previous series.

Pieces dated 1921 are very scarce; only about 100 are known. According to Fred Bowman (see Bibliography), almost the entire striking of over 200,000 remained unissued until 1928, when it was melted. Those that escaped the melting pot are at least in part ones (a) sold by the Mint to visitors (b) sold to those ordering 1921 year sets (c) given to various individuals as part of 1921 specimen sets.

Diameter: 29.72 mm; weight: 11.620 grams; composition 1911-19: .925 silver, .075 copper; 1920-36: .800 silver, .200 copper; edge: reeded.

     Obverse 1911   Obverse 1912-1936   Reverse 1911-1936

     G. — *Band of crown worn through.*
     V.G. — *Band of crown worn through at highest point.*
     Fine — *Jewels in band of crown will be blurred.*
     V.F. — *Band of crown still clear but no longer sharp.*
     E.F. — *Band of crown slightly worn but generally sharp and clear.*

"Godless" Obverse (1911)

| 1911............209,972 | | 4.00 | 9.00 | 35.00 | 125.00 | 425.00 | 750.00 |

Date	Quan. Minted	Good	V.G.	Fine	V.F.	E.F.	Unc.
Modified Obverse Legend (1912-1936)							
1912............285,867	$1.10	$2.25	$4.50	$13.00	$45.00	$300.00
1913............265,889	1.10	2.25	4.50	13.00	45.00	275.00
1914............160,128	1.50	3.50	6.00	17.50	60.00	375.00
1916............459,070	1.00	1.75	2.75	7.50	25.00	200.00
1917............752,213	.90	1.10	2.00	6.00	22.50	175.00
1918............854,989	.90	1.10	2.00	6.00	22.50	175.00
1919..........1,113,429	.90	1.10	2.00	6.00	22.50	175.00
1920............584,691	.90	1.10	2.00	6.00	22.50	175.00
1921............206,398		2,700	3,250	4,000	5,000	6,500
1929............228,328	.80	1.00	1.75	6.00	15.00	175.00
1931............57,581	2.25	5.00	10.00	15.00	55.00	350.00
1932............19,213	15.00	27.50	45.00	90.00	250.00	700.00
1934............39,539	2.50	5.50	10.00	20.00	70.00	400.00
1936............38,550	2.50	5.50	10.00	20.00	55.00	225.00

George VI Coinage 1937-1952

There are two obverses, both of which have the bare-headed portrait of the King by T. H. Paget (H.P. below). The varieties differ in that the second (1948-52) incorporated the change in the King's titles which ensued when India was granted independence from England (see text on the 1 cent).

In keeping with a Government decision to modernize all reverses, a simplified Canadian coat of arms was chosen for this denomination. The simplification involved omission of the crest, helmet and mantling, motto and floral emblems; in addition, no attempt was made to heraldically color the shield and banners. The shield consists of the arms of England (three lions), Scotland (rearing lion), royalist France (three fleurs-de-lis) and Ireland (a harp) and is surmounted by a stylized Imperial crown. At the left is the English lion holding a lance with the Union flag; on the right is a Scottish unicorn holding a lance with the flag of royalist France. The whole is resting upon a layer of serried clouds. The initials K.G. flanking the crown indicate the designer, George Kruger-Gray.

The position of the final digit in the date varies because during most of the 1940's it was punched separately into each die. Such varieties are too minor to include in a catalog of this kind.

1946 and 1949 "hoof." These items are apparently the products of damaged dies and as such are not true die varieties. For further comments on such items, see pg. 7.

1947 maple leaf and 7 varieties. The 1947 (no maple leaf) issue comes with two styles of 7 in the date. One is a rather tall figure, the bottom of which points to the left and the other is a shorter 7 with the bottom curving back to the right. Both 7's were also used for the maple leaf issue (see 1 cent text) struck in 1948.

1950 no lines in 0. In 1950 the 50 cents dies were derived from a single, fully dated matrix in which the 0 of the date had 4 horizontal lines in its center. Depending upon the amount of polishing or re-polishing (see pg. 6) of each individual die, the lines in the 0 ranged from completely present to partially missing to entirely absent. Previous catalogers have chosen to list as a separate entry those pieces that lack the lines. For further comments on such items, see pg. 6.

Diameter: 29.72 mm; weight: 11.620 grams; composition: .800 silver, .200 copper; edge: reeded.

George VI 1936-1952

V.G. — No detail in hair above the ear.

Fine — Only slight detail in hair above the ear.

V.F. — Where not worn the hair is clear but not sharp.

E.F. — Slight wear in the hair over the ear.

Date	Quan. Minted	V.G.	Fine	V.F.	E.F.	Unc.
ET IND: IMP: *Obverse (1937-1947)*						
1937	192,016	$2.00	$3.00	$4.00	$5.50	$17.50
1938	192,018	2.50	3.50	5.00	27.50	100.00
1939	287,976	1.75	2.75	4.00	5.50	30.00
1940	1,996,566	.80	1.25	1.75	3.00	12.00
1941	1,714,874	.80	1.25	1.75	3.00	14.00
1942	1,974,165	.75	1.00	1.50	3.00	14.00
1943	3,109,583	.75	1.00	1.50	3.00	12.00
1944	2,460,205	.75	1.00	1.50	3.00	12.00
1945	1,959,528	.75	1.00	1.50	3.00	11.00

		"Hoof" in 6	Tall 7	Short 7	Tall 7	Short 7
			Without maple leaf		With maple leaf after date	
1946 normal 6	}950,235		.75	1.00	1.50	3.00	25.00
"hoof" in 6			4.00	8.00	15.00	25.00	110.00
1947 tall 7	}424,885		1.50	3.00	4.50	6.50	45.00
short 7			1.25	2.50	3.25	5.00	40.00
1947 maple leaf, tall 7	}38,433		12.50	17.50	25.00	30.00	65.00
maple leaf, short 7			200.00	275.00	350.00	475.00	700.00

Obverse 1948-1952

"Hoof" over 9

Lines in 0

No lines in 0

Date	Quan. Minted	V.G.	Fine	V.F.	E.F.	Unc.
Modified Obverse Legend (1948-1952)						
1948...................	37,784	$20.00	$25.00	$30.00	$35.00	$70.00
1949 normal 9..........	858,991	.75	1.00	1.50	2.50	10.00
"hoof" over 9......		1.75	2.75	4.50	7.50	60.00
1950 lines in 0........	2,384,179	.70	.75	.95	1.50	7.00
no lines in 0......		2.50	3.00	4.00	7.00	55.00
1951.................	2,421,730	.70	.75	.80	1.25	6.00
1952.................	2,596,465	.70	.75	.80	1.25	5.00

Elizabeth II Laureate Bust, Old Arms 1953-1958

The initial obverse for the 1953 issue had a high relief portrait by Mrs. Mary Gillick (M.G. on truncation) which did not strike up well on the coins. Later in the year, the relief was lowered and the hair and shoulder detail re-engraved. On the second variety two lines at the shoulder, representing a fold in the Queen's gown, are clear, while on the first variety they are almost missing. The obverses also differ in the shape of some letters and in positioning of the legend relative to the rim denticles (see the 1 cent text for more details).

The first reverse for the 1953 issue, used only with the high relief "no shoulder fold" obverse, is identical to that used for the 1950-52 George VI coinages, both in the device and the style and size of the date. Later in the year a new reverse with a larger date and with design elements positioned closer to the rim denticles was introduced. The second reverse is associated with both the high and low relief obverses, the former combination being a mule. In an attempt to reduce the "ghosting" that had been so common in the past, a third modification was introduced in 1955. It is characterized by smaller design elements.

Diameter: 29.72 mm; weight: 11.620 grams; composition: .800 silver, .200 copper; edge: reeded.

Large coat of arms   Smaller coat of arms
1953-1954   1955-1958

No shoulder fold 1953   With shoulder fold 1953-1964

Fine — Leaves worn almost through; shoulder straps indistinct.
V.F. — Leaves considerably worn; shoulder straps must show.
E.F. — Laurel leaves on the head somewhat worn.

Small date 1953   Large date 1953-1954

Date	Quan. Minted	V.G.	Fine	V.F.	E.F.	Unc.
Small Date Reverse (1953)						
1953 no sh. fold........1,630,429		$ .70	$ .75	$ .80	$1.25	$7.50
Large Date Reverse (1953-1954)						
1953 no sh. fold..... ⎫ Incl. above		5.00	10.00	17.50	32.50	55.00
with sh. fold.... ⎭		.75	.90	1.25	3.00	25.00
1954................506,305		.70	.90	1.25	2.00	17.50
Smaller Coat of Arms (1955-1958)						
1955................753,511		.70	.85	1.00	2.00	7.00
1956..............1,379,499				.70	1.00	4.50
1957..............2,171,689				.65	.90	3.75
1958..............2,957,266				.60	.85	3.00

Complete Coat of Arms Reverse 1959-1964

The obverse for the 1959-64 issues continued to be the shoulder fold variety.

In 1957 the Canadian coat of arms as described by the Royal proclamation of 21 November, 1921 (except for the replacement of the Imperial crown with the St. Edward's crown, which Elizabeth preferred) was approved for all government purposes. A representation of the complete coat of arms was consequently modeled and engraved by Thomas Shingles (TS flanking lower part of shield) for this denomination. As far as was practical, considering the size of the coins, heraldic coloring of the arms and the flags was attempted: blue is represented by horizontal lines, while white or silver is plain with no symbols. On the 1959 issue the background of the lower section (the Canadian emblem) in the shield was inadvertently colored blue, instead of the correct white or silver. The lines were removed beginning with the 1960 issue and no further changes were made in the reverse until 1967. Physical specifications remained as for the previous issues.

Horizontal lines in
lower shield 1959

No lines in lower
shield 1960-1966

Date	Quan. Minted	E.F.	Unc.
"Blue Lower Panel" Reverse (1959)			
1959	3,095,535	$ .85	$3.00
"White Lower Panel" Reverse (1960-1966)			
1960	3,488,897	.75	2.50
1961	3,584,417	.60	1.50
1962	5,208,030	.60	1.50
1963	8,348,871	.60	.75
1964	9,377,676	.60	.75

Elizabeth II, Tiara Obverse 1965-

In 1965 an obverse with a new style portrait by Arnold Machin was introduced. The Queen has more mature facial features and is wearing a tiara. The reverse and physical specifications continued as previously.

1965	12,629,974	.60	.75
1966	7,683,228	.60	.75

Confederation Centennial 1967

All denominations for 1967 bore special reverses to commemorate the 1867 confederation of the provinces of Canada, Nova Scotia and New Brunswick to form the Dominion of Canada. The design, by Alex Colville, shows a howling wolf.

1967 Confederation commem.	4,211,395	1.00	3.25

Coat of Arms Reverse Resumed 1968-

With the resumption of the regular reverse design in 1968, two significant changes were made. The diameter and weight were reduced, and the composition changed to nickel.

Diameter: 27.13 mm; weight: 8.099 grams; composition: 1.000 nickel; edge: reeded.

Date	Quan. Minted	E.F.	Unc.
1968	3,966,932		$ .75
1969	7,113,929		.75
1970			.75

1 DOLLAR
George V Silver Jubilee Commemorative 1935

The first Canadian dollar issued for circulation had a special obverse to mark the 25th anniversary of the accession of George V. The portrait was from a model by Percy Metcalfe, used previously for the obverses of certain Australian and New Zealand coinages of 1933-35. The Latin legend is translated: "George V, King, Emperor; Regnal year 25."

The reverse device consists of a canoe manned by an Indian and a *voyageur* (traveling agent of a fur company), behind which is an islet with two trees. In the sky are lines representing the northern lights. On the front bundle in the canoe are the incuse initials HB; these signify Hudson's Bay Co., which played an important role in Canada's early history. The designer was Emmanuel Hahn (EH at left under canoe).

Diameter: 35.99 mm; weight: 23.328 grams; composition: .800 silver, .200 copper; edge: reeded.

V.G. — *Band of the crown is worn through at the highest point.*
Fine — *Jewels in the band of crown will be blurred.*
V.F. — *Band of the crown still clear but no longer sharp.*
E.F — *Band of the crown slightly worn but generally sharp and clear.*

Date	Quan. Minted	V.G.	Fine	V.F.	E.F.	A.U.	Unc.
1935 Silver Jubilee	428,707	$5.00	$8.00	$10.50	$13.00	$15.00	$26.00

George V Regular Issue 1936

The obverse for 1936 had the regular design for George V, first seen on the 1 through 50 cent business strikes in 1912. The designer was Sir E. B. Mac-Kennal (B.M. on truncation). The master matrix from which the 1936 obverse dies were prepared was that made in 1911 for the dollar proposed at that time.

The reverse design, physical specifications and grading are as for the 1935 issue.

Date	Quan. Minted	V.G.	Fine	V.F.	E.F.	A.U.	Unc.
1936............306,100		$4.00	$7.50	$9.00	$11.00	$14.00	$26.00

George VI, Voyageur Reverse 1937-1938

The obverse has the conventional bare-headed portrait of the King by T. H. Paget (H.P. under rear of neck) as used for the lower denominations.

The reverse remains unchanged from the George V issues.

Diameter: 35.99 mm; weight: 23.328 grams; composition: .800 silver, .200 copper; edge: reeded.

V.G. — No detail in hair above ear.
Fine — Only slight detail in hair above ear.
V.F. — Where not worn, hair is clear but not sharp.
E.F. — Slight wear in hair over ear.

1937............241,002	3.00	5.50	7.50	10.00	12.50	26.50
1938............90,304	4.50	10.00	13.00	16.00	22.50	40.00

Royal Visit Commemorative 1939

In 1939 a special reverse was used on the dollar to mark the visit of George VI and Queen Elizabeth to Canada. The design shows the center block of the Parliament buildings in Ottawa. Above is the Latin phrase FIDE SUORUM REGNAT, meaning "He reigns by the faith of his people." The designer was Emmanuel Hahn; his initials EH flanked the building on the original model, but were removed by government decision prior to the manufacture of the dies. Because of lack of demand, about 150,000 specimens were returned to the Mint and melted in 1940.

The obverse design and physical specifications are as for the 1937-38 issues.

Date	Quan. Minted	V.G.	Fine	V.F.	E.F.	A.U.	Unc.
1939 R. Visit...	1,363,816	$1.50	$3.75	$5.00	$6.00	$8.00	$15.00

Voyageur Reverse Resumed 1945-1948

During 1945-48 two major obverse varieties appeared on this and all lower denominations. The first has the usual legend containing ET IND: IMP: ("and Emperor of India") and the second has that phrase deleted (see text on the 1 cent for more details).

The reverse design and physical specifications are as on the 1937-38 issues.

1947 varieties. The 1947 issue of the dollar has two styles of 7 which differ mainly in the lower tip of the 7 in the date. The 1947 maple leaf coins of 1948 (see the 1 cent text) have only one of these 7's.

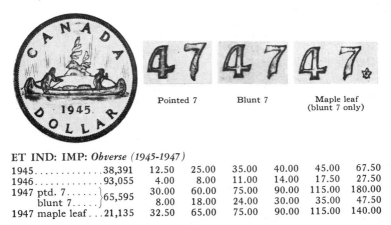

Pointed 7   Blunt 7   Maple leaf (blunt 7 only)

ET IND: IMP: *Obverse (1945-1947)*

1945.............	38,391	12.50	25.00	35.00	40.00	45.00	67.50
1946.............	93,055	4.00	8.00	11.00	14.00	17.50	27.50
1947 ptd. 7......	⎫65,595	30.00	60.00	75.00	90.00	115.00	180.00
blunt 7.....	⎭	8.00	18.00	24.00	30.00	35.00	47.50
1947 maple leaf...21,135		32.50	65.00	75.00	90.00	115.00	140.00

Date	Quan. Minted	V.G.	Fine	V.F.	E.F.	A.U.	Unc.

Modified Obverse Legend (1948-1952)

Date	Quan. Minted	V.G.	Fine	V.F.	E.F.	A.U.	Unc.
1948	18,780	$50.00	$110.00	$140.00	$170.00	$200.00	$250.00

Newfoundland Commemorative 1949

On 31 December 1949 Newfoundland became a province of the Dominion of Canada. To mark this event a special reverse appeared on the dollar for that year. The *Matthew,* the ship in which John Cabot is thought to have discovered Newfoundland, is depicted. Below is the Latin phrase FLOREAT TERRA NOVA, "May the new found land flourish." Thomas Shingles was the designer and engraver (T.S. above horizon at right); he engraved the master matrix entirely by hand. The obverse is as the 1948 issue, and the physical specifications remain unchanged.

Date	Quan. Minted	Fine	V.F.	E.F.	A.U.	Unc.
1949 New'land comm	672,218	6.00	7.50	9.00	10.00	15.00

Voyageur Reverse Resumed 1950-1952

The obverse for the final George VI Voyageurs is as on the 1948-49 issues. There are two noteworthy reverse varieties. The first is the usual "water lines" variety, used for all Voyageurs prior to 1950. The second is the so-called "no water lines" reverse of 1952. On this interesting variety the water lines on both sides of the canoe have been removed and the right-hand tip of the islet re-engraved so that it is both wider and longer than before. There can be no question that the "no water lines" was a deliberate issue; furthermore, unlike the "Arnpriors" (see below) it was created by the alteration of a matrix — not simply an individual die or dies. For some reason the modification was apparently not acceptable because it was used only during the one year.

"Arnprior" dollars of 1950 and 1955. In 1955 a firm in Arnprior, Ontario ordered and received 2,000 silver dollars for use as Christmas bonuses. It was later discovered that these coins had only 1½ water lines (instead of the normal 3) to the right of the canoe. This difference became popular and was collected separately from the "normal" counterpart. Further study revealed that some dollars of 1950, 1951 and perhaps 1952-53 have a similar water line configuration. Only the 1950 and 1955's are currently included in the major listings. These items are the result of inadvertent overpolishing of individual dies and as such are *not* true die varieties. In fact, for 1950, 1955 and certain other years there is a whole gamut of water line differences, ranging from 3 full lines to parts of all 3 to 1½. Collectors and catalogers have tended to deem all partial water lines greater than 1½ as normal. Whether items like this have any place in a more general catalog is very questionable; they are included here only because of their current popularity. For further comments on such issues, see pg. 6.

Physical specifications are as on the previous issues.

3 water lines, small islet tip (normal 1935-1952)	1½ water lines 1950	No water lines, 1952

Date	Quan. Minted	Fine	V.F.	E.F.	A.U.	Unc.
"Water Lines" Reverse (1950-1952)						
1950, 3 lines............ } 1½ lns. "Arnprior" }	261,002	$3.00 20.00	$5.00 25.00	$6.00 35.00	$7.50 45.00	$12.00 60.00
1951.................416,395		3.00	4.00	4.75	5.50	11.00
1952.................406,148		3.00	3.75	4.75	5.50	11.00
"No Water Lines" Reverse (1952)						
1952...............Incl. above		4.00	6.00	6.75	10.00	15.00

Elizabeth II, Laureate Bust 1953-1964

The first obverse for 1953 had a high relief, laureate portrait of the Queen by Mrs. Mary Gillick (M.G. on truncation) which did not strike up well on the coins. Later in the year the rim width and coin diameter were increased, the relief lowered and the hair and shoulder detail re-engraved. The latter included sharpening two lines which represented a fold in the Queen's gown. The two varieties also differ in positioning of the legend relative to rim denticles and the styles of some letters.

The reverse used with the "no shoulder fold" obverse on 1953 was the "water lines" George VI variety. It has a very narrow rim and the triangular islet tip extending to the canoe's right ends about halfway to the rim denticles. Together with the obverse change came a slightly modified reverse, the most distinctive of which are a wider rim and a right-hand islet tip that extends almost to the rim denticles.

1955 Arnprior. See pg. 61.

1957 1 water line. This item had the same cause as the "Arnpriors" (see above) and is therefore not a true die variety.

Diameter 1953 narrow rim: 35.99 mm; 1953 wide rim - 1964: 36.07 mm; weight: 23.328 grams; composition: .800 silver, .200 copper; edge: reeded.

No shoulder fold 1953

With shoulder fold 1953-1964

Narrow rim, short islet tip 1953

Fine — Leaves worn almost through.
V.F. — Leaves considerably worn.
E.F. — Laurel leaves on the head somewhat worn.

Date	Quan. Minted	Fine	V.F.	E.F.	A.U.	Unc.
Narrow Rim Reverse (1953)						
1953 no sh. fold........1,074,578		$1.75	$2.25	$3.00	$5.00	$7.00
Wide Rim Reverse (1953-1957)						
1953 with sh. fold.....Incl. above		1.75	2.25	3.00	5.00	7.00
1954....................246,606		3.75	5.00	7.00	9.25	15.50

"Arnprior" water lines (overpolished die) 1955

1 water line (overpolished die) 1957

Date	Quan. Minted	Fine	V.F.	E.F.	A.U.	Unc.
1955 "normal" w. lines..	} 268,105	$3.75	$5.00	$7.00	$9.25	$15.50
"Arnprior"........		30.00	40.00	45.00	50.00	62.50
1956.................	209,092	4.50	6.00	7.50	11.00	19.00
1957 "normal" w. lines..	} 496,389	2.00	2.50	3.25	4.00	6.00
one water line.....		4.00	6.00	7.50	9.50	14.00

British Columbia Commemorative 1958

To commemorate the gold rush centenary and establishment of British Columbia as an English Crown colony, a special reverse by Stephen Trenka (ST at right bottom of totem) was employed. British Columbia is the only area in Canada where the Indians constructed totem poles, so the design is very appropriate. It was rumored that the issue was unpopular with the coastal Indians because it contained an element which to them signified death. The physical specifications remained unchanged.

1958 Brit. Columbia....3,039,630	2.75	3.00	3.50	4.25	5.50

Voyageur Reverse Resumed 1959-1963

There are two major varieties of the Voyageur reverse during this period. The first is the wide rim design, introduced in late 1953. The second has re-engraved water lines and northern lights.

Reverse of 1953-1957 (1959)

1959........................1,443,502	1.75	2.00	2.50	3.00

Recut Water Lines and Northern Lights (1960-1963)

1960........................1,420,486	1.75	2.00	2.50	3.00
1961........................1,262,231			2.00	2.75
1962........................1,884,789			2.00	2.75
1963........................4,179,981			1.60	2.00

Confederation Meetings Commemorative 1964

To mark the 100th anniversary of the meetings at Charlottetown, Prince Edward Island and Quebec, P.Q. which paved the way for Confederation, a special reverse was used for the dollar in 1964. The device is a circle within which are the conjoined French fleur-de-lis, Irish shamrock, Scottish thistle and English rose. Although Dinko Vodanovic was the designer, the Royal Canadian Mint's chief engraver, Thomas Shingles, actually prepared the model based on Vodanovic's sketch. The initials of both men (D.V. and T.S.) appear along the inner cirlce.

The obverse of this issue has a re-engraved portrait. It is by Myron Cook, modifying Shingle's alteration of the original Gillick design. The new features consist mostly of sharpened gown details. Physical specifications remained unchanged.

Date	Quan. Minted	A.U.	Unc.
1964 Meetings...............................	7,296,832	$1.60	$2.00

Elizabeth II, Tiara Obverse 1965-1966

In 1965 a new obverse portrait by Arnold Machin was introduced. The Queen has more mature facial features and is wearing a tiara. Three obverse varieties exist for 1965. The first has a flat field and small rim beads, and was replaced because of unacceptable die life. The second variety has a slightly concave field, medium sized rim beads and slight changes in the portrait. Most distinctive is a very thin support to the rearmost jewel. This variety was struck from a single "test die," made to determine whether a concave field would give better die life. The experiment was successful and a new matrix, punches and dies were prepared. Coins from these dies have the concave field and rim beads even larger than on the "test" variety. In addition, the medium and large beads varieties differ in the positioning of the legend relative to the rim beads.

The 1965-66 reverse is very similar but not identical to earlier Voyageurs. Physical specifications remain unchanged.

1965 date and combinational varieties. Coupled with the small and large beads obverses were two reverses, having trivially different 5's in the dates. The medium beads obverse is coupled with only one of the 5's.

Small and large   Medium bead
bead obverse   obverse
Detail of rear jewel in tiara

Pointed 5

Blunt 5

Small beads   Medium beads   Large beads

Date	Quan. Minted	A.U.	Unc.
1965 sm. beads, pointed 5 . . . . .var. 1		$1.60	$2.00
sm. beads, blunt 5 . . . . .var. 2		1.60	2.00
med. beads, pointed 5 . . . . .var. 5	10,768,569	2.75	10.00
lg. beads, pointed 5 . . . . .var. 3		1.75	2.50
lg. beads, blunt 5 . . . . .var. 4		1.60	2.00
1966 sm. beads obverse	9,912,178	1.50	1.60
lg. beads obverse		1.50	1.60

Confederation Centennial 1967

All denominations for 1967 bore special reverses to commemorate the 1867 confederation of the provinces of Canada, Nova Scotia and New Brunswick to form the Dominion of Canada. The designer was Alex Colville; the device shows a Canada goose in flight.

1967 Confederation commemorative 6,767,496 2.00 3.25

Voyageur Reverse Resumed 1968-1969

With the resumption of the regular reverse design in 1968, two significant changes were made. The diameter and weight were reduced and the composition changed to nickel.

Diameter: 32.13 mm; weight: 15.616 grams; composition: 1.000 nickel; edge: reeded.

Date	Quan. Minted	A.U.	Unc.
1968	5,579,714		$1.50
1969	4,809,313		1.50

Manitoba Centennial 1970

This denomination bore a special reverse in 1970 to mark the 100th anniversary of Manitoba's entrance into the Dominion of Canada. Raymond Taylor was the designer (RT to the right of the center stem); the device depicts the prairie crocus, Manitoba's flower. Physical specifications are as for the 1968-69 issues.

1970 Manitoba commemorative.........................   1.75

British Columbia Centennial 1971

A dollar has been announced to honor the 100th anniversary of British Columbia's entry into the Confederation in 1870. The coin will bear a special reverse design, but in all other respects will be identical to the coins of 1968 through 1970.

GOLD 5 DOLLARS
George V Coinage 1912-1914

The obverse of this brief series was derived from the portrait model of the King by Sir E. B. MacKennal (B.M. on truncation).

For the reverse was selected a design that is still considered one of the most beautiful on Canadian coins. The device consists of the shield from the Canadian coat of arms as granted by Queen Victoria in a Royal Warrant of 26 May 1868, behind which are crossed boughs of maple. The quartered shield has the arms of the four provinces which originally formed the Dominion. These arms are: St. George's cross above, three maple leaves below (Ontario); two fleurs-de-lis above, lion in center, three maple leaves below (Quebec); a lion above, ancient galley below (New Brunswick); two thistles above, salmon in center, single thistle below (Nova Scotia).

Diameter: 21.59 mm; weight: 8.359 grams; composition: .900 gold, .100 copper; edge: reeded.

Fine — Jewels in the band of crown will be blurred.

V.F. — Band of the crown is still clear but no longer sharp.

E.F. — Band of the crown slightly worn but generally sharp and clear.

Date	Quan. Minted	Fine	V.F.	E.F.	Unc.
1912	165,680	$50.00	$60.00	$70.00	$80.00
1913	98,823	50.00	60.00	72.50	80.00
1914	31,122	175.00	225.00	250.00	325.00

GOLD 10 DOLLARS
George V Coinage 1912-1914

The obverse was derived from the well known portrait model of the King by Sir E. B. MacKennal (B.M. on truncation).

The reverse, designed and engraved by W. H. J. Blakemore, is very similar to that on the five dollars described above. It is worth noting that the Canadian government also wanted to have additional gold denominations for George V. This is evidenced by a letter dated 10 November 1910 from the Master of the Royal Canadian Mint to the Royal Mint in London requesting that matrices and punches be prepared for ". . . $20 gold, $10 gold, $5 gold, $2½ gold . . ." Obviously, plans were altered and only the $5 and $10 denominations were actually issued.

Diameter: 26.92 mm; weight: 16.718 grams; composition: .900 gold, .100 copper; edge: reeded.

1912	74,759	90.00	110.00	125.00	160.00
1913	149,232	90.00	110.00	135.00	175.00
1914	140,068	110.00	140.00	160.00	190.00

GOLD 20 DOLLARS
Elizabeth II, Confederation Centennial 1967

This denomination was struck only for the special proof sets of Confederation centennial coins, which were originally sold in a black leather box to the public for $40. It is the only coin of the set that does not have the commemorative dates "1867-1967." The obverse is Arnold Machin's design, introduced on regular denominations in 1965, and the reverse is an adaption of the Canadian coat of arms by Myron Cook, using Thomas Shingles' model for the 50 cents type of 1959.

Diameter: 27.05 mm; weight: 18.274 grams; composition: .900 gold, .100 copper; edge: reeded.

Date	Quan. Minted		Proof
1967................337,512		Issued only in proof set.	$50.00

OTTAWA MINT GOLD SOVEREIGNS

Like other branches of the Royal Mint, the Ottawa Mint was authorized to strike gold sovereigns, and did so during the period 1908-19. The designs and physical specifications were identical to those of the corresponding English issues, except for the presence of the C mint mark for Canada just above the date on the Ottawa strikings. Sovereigns struck in London had no mint mark, while pieces with mint marks I, M, P, S and SA were from mints in India, Australia and South Africa.

During the First World War, these coins were used to help pay for war materials that England purchased from the United States. England was thus saved the risk of sending London-minted gold across the Atlantic.

Such "branch mint" sovereigns are generally considered to form part of the coinage of the country in which they were struck, and so are included here.

Edward VII Coinage 1908-1910

The obverse was derived from a portrait model by G. W. De Saulles (DES. below neck) and the reverse is a slight modification of the original 1816 St. George and the dragon design by Benedetto Pistrucci (B.P. at lower right).

Diameter: 22.05 mm; weight: 7.988 grams; composition: .917 gold, .083 copper; edge: reeded.

Position of C mint mark
for Ottawa Mint

Date	Quan. Minted	Fine	V.F.	E.F.	Unc.
1908C	636	$450.00	$550.00	$675.00	$750.00
1909C	16,273	60.00	75.00	85.00	100.00
1910C	28,012	60.00	75.00	85.00	100.00

George V Coinage 1911-1919

The obverse was derived from a portrait model by Sir E. B. MacKennal (B.M. on truncation) and the reverse is as on the Edward VII issues.

1916C. Despite the reported mintage of over 6,000, specimens of this date are extremely rare, with less than 10 known today. The basis for this discrepancy remains a mystery.

Diameter: 22.05 mm; weight: 7.988 grams; composition: .917 gold, .083 copper; edge: reeded.

Fine — *Little detail in the hair above the ear and beard is considerably worn.*

V.F. — *Wear on the head spreads nearer the ear and slight wear develops on the beard.*

E.F. — *Hair over the ear is only slightly worn. Beard is still sharp.*

1911C	256,946	20.00	25.00	30.00	32.50
1913C	3,715	375.00	500.00	625.00	850.00
1914C	14,891	75.00	85.00	95.00	110.00
1916C	6,111	—	—	—	—
1917C	58,845	20.00	25.00	30.00	35.00
1918C	106,516	20.00	25.00	30.00	35.00
1919C	135,889	20.00	25.00	30.00	35.00

PROOFLIKE MINT SETS AND DOLLARS

In 1949 the Royal Canadian Mint's numismatic section was established. During 1949-1953 it was not only possible to obtain mint sets of the current year, but sometimes those of previous years as well. These coins initially came in cellophane envelopes and later in a white card wrapped in cellophane, and almost all were *regular production strikes* of the same quality as those placed in bags and sent out for general use. However, *a few* of the sets and dollars or at least the period 1951-53 had a markedly superior finish (but are not of specimen quality); in 1954 dealer J. E. Charlton introduced the term "proof-like" to describe one such 1953 set. These special coins represented the modest beginning of the Mint's attempts to produce higher quality strikings in quantity for collectors. Selected dies and planchets are used and the coins are more carefully struck than the regular issues.

Beginning in 1954, all sets and dollars sold to collectors by the Mint have been the specially prepared "prooflike" coins. Their quality has generally been good; however, in 1965 and again in 1968-69 difficulties in producing a good surface on the coins was encountered. The packaging for the sets changed from cardboard in cellophane to a sealed pliofilm pouch beginning in 1961. Each pouch has ROYAL CANADIAN MINT impressed into the dividing areas.

In most years it has been possible to order dollars separately; in other years collectors have removed them from the full mint sets.

It should be noted that "prooflike" is not an official term; the Mint simply calls these coins "uncirculated coin." Information about purchasing current year sets and single dollars can be obtained by writing to: Coins Uncirculated, P.O. Box 470, Ottawa 2, Ontario, Canada.

| | | QUANTITY MINTED | | VALUE | |
| | | 6-Coin Set | Dollar Only | 6-Coin Set | Dollar Only |
Date	Set				
1951 both 5¢; 7 coin set......		*	*	$80.00	$40.00
1952 no water lines dollar....		*	*	90.00	50.00
water lines dollar.......		*	*	80.00	40.00
1953 no shoulder fold obv.'s..		*	*	80.00	40.00
shoulder fold obv.'s.....		*	*	300.00	100.00
1954 no shoulder fold 1¢.....		**7,426	**1,268	140.00	37.50
shoulder fold 1¢........				85.00	
1955 "Normal" dollar.......		**6,301	**5,501	70.00	37.50
"Arnprior" dollar.......				100.00	80.00
1956......................		**9,018	**6,154	30.00	17.50
1957......................		**11,862	**4,379	27.50	15.00
1958......................		18,259	14,978	30.00	14.00
1959......................		31,577	13,583	15.00	6.00
1960......................		64,097	18,631	10.00	5.00
1961......................		98,373	22,555	10.00	5.00
1962......................		200,950	47,591	5.00	3.00
1963......................		673,006	290,529	3.25	2.75
1964......................		1,653,162	1,209,279	3.00	1.50
1965 pointed 5 dollar........		2,904,352	——	2.25	1.50
blunt 5 dollar..........				2.50	1.75
1966......................		672,514	——	3.50	2.25
1967......................		963,714	——	7.50	4.50
1968......................		521,641	885,124	3.25	2.00
1969......................		326,203	211,112	4.75	2.00
1970 separate dollar is cased..				6.00	2.75

*Unknown.
**Estimated.

3

THE FRENCH REGIME

None of the coins of the French regime is strictly Canadian. They were all general issues for the French colonies of the New World. The coinage of 1670 was authorized by an edict of Louis XIV dated February 19, 1670, for use in New France, Acadia, the French settlements in Newfoundland, and the French West Indies. The copper of 1717 to 1722 was authorized by edicts of 1716 and 1721 for use in New France, Louisiana, and the French West Indies.

Issue of 1670

The coinage of 1670 consisted of silver 5 and 15 sols. A copper 2 deniers was also authorized but never struck. A total of 200,000 of the 5 sols was struck, and 40,000 of the 15 sols, at Paris. Nantes was to have coined the copper, but did not; the reasons for this may never be known, since the archives of the Nantes mint before 1700 were destroyed. The only known specimen is a pattern struck at Paris. The silver coins were raised in value by a third in 1672 to keep them circulating, but in vain. They rapidly disappeared, and by 1680 none was to be seen. Later they were restored to their original value.

Copper

		V.G.	Fine	V.F.	E.F.	Unc.
1	Double or 2 deniers 1670 . .			Unique		

Silver

		V.G.	Fine	V.F.	E.F.	Unc.
2	5 sols 1670	$100.00	$200.00	$300.00	$450.00	$600.00
3	15 sols 1670.	1,500	2,000	3,000	4,000	6,000

Coinage of 1717-1720

The copper 6 and 12 deniers of 1717 were authorized by an edict of Louis XV dated December 1716, to be struck at Perpignan. The order could not be carried out, for the supply of copper was too brassy. A second attempt in 1720 also failed, probably for the same reason. All these coins are extremely rare, the 6 deniers of 1720 probably being unique.

Copper

		V.G.	Fine	V.F.	E.F.	Unc.
4	6 deniers 1717............	$1,000	$1,500	$2,000	—	—
5	6 deniers 1720............			Unique		
6	12 deniers 1717...........	1,500	2,000	3,000	4,000	—

Coinage of 1721-1722

The copper coinage of 1721-1722 was authorized by an edict of Louis XV dated June 1721. The coins were struck on copper blanks imported from Sweden. Rouen and La Rochelle struck pieces of 9 deniers in 1721 and 1722. New France received 534,000 pieces, mostly from the mint of La Rochelle, but only 8,180 were successfully put into circulation as the colonists disliked copper. In 1726 the rest of the issue was sent back to France.

Copper

1722, 2 over 1

7	9 deniers 1721B..........	50.00	75.00	100.00	150.00	—
8	9 deniers 1721H..........	25.00	35.00	40.00	50.00	—
9	9 deniers 1722H, 2 over 1..	50.00	75.00	100.00	150.00	—
9a	9 deniers 1722H, norm. date	30.00	45.00	60.00	75.00	—

French Billon Coins used in Canada

These coins were issued for use in France and all French colonies. Large shipments were sent to Canada.

Almost every type of French coin minted between 1600 and 1759 sooner or later found its way into Canada. To enumerate all these would be unwise, and therefore we have confined the listings to the billon coinages, shipments of which were known to have been sent to Canada. The "John Law" coinage, cataloged as Canadian by Leroux, was definitely not intended for the French colonies when it was first coined. It is a coinage which was issued for France at an inflated value during the period of John Law's financial schemes. After the crash of 1720 and the ensuing deflation, the coins were permitted to circulate in the colonies as well.

11

		V.G.	Fine	V.F.	E.F.	Unc.
10	15 deniers 1710-1713AA...	$40.00	$70.00	$90.00	$125.00	$175.00
11	30 deniers 1709-1713AA...	20.00	30.00	50.00	75.00	150.00
12	30 deniers 1709-1713D.....	20.00	30.00	50.00	75.00	150.00

13	Half sol marque 1738-54...	35.00	50.00	65.00	90.00	150.00
14	Sol marque 1738-1760.....	10.00	20.00	30.00	45.00	65.00

The piece of 30 deniers was called a *mousquetaire,* and was coined at Metz and Lyons. The 15 deniers was coined only at Metz. The sol marque and half were coined at almost every French mint, those of Paris being commonest. Only Paris coined the half sol after 1748. Specimens of the sol marque dated after 1760 were not used in Canada, which by then was firmly in British hands.

Mint marks on French Regime coins:

A...............Paris	D...............Lyons
AA..............Metz	H.........La Rochelle
B...............Rouen	Q............Perpignan

4

ANONYMOUS and MISCELLANEOUS TOKENS

These pieces are of English or Irish origin, some of which had been used in the British Isles before being sent to Canada. Those of light weight were probably struck on Canadian order. A few, such as the North American token, circulated to a limited extent in the United States near the Canadian border.

The North American Token

The North American token was struck in Dublin long after 1781. It was dated 1781 to evade Canadian laws against the importation of anonymous tokens after 1825. To add to the illusion of age, the coin was struck without a collar.

		V.G.	Fine	V.F.	E.F.	Unc.
15	North American Token, copper..............	$6.00	$7.50	$9.00	$12.00	$50.00
15a	Same, brass.............	8.00	10.00	12.00	18.00	65.00

The Success to Trade Token

Number 16 is an anonymous English piece with altered legends. The phrase "Success to Trade" was struck over "George III Rules," and "Commerce" was struck over "Britannia."

16	Success to Trade.........	7.00	10.00	15.00	20.00	50.00

Other Isssues

The pieces numbered 17 through 21 and 23 were engraved by Thomas Halliday and struck in Birmingham. The "Irish" piece, number 17, evidently was used in Ireland before being sent to Canada, for specimens have been found there.

	V.G.	Fine	V.F.	E.F.	Unc.
17 Irishman, Pure Copper Preferable to Paper.....	$3.00	$5.00	$7.00	$10.00	$40.00

18   19   20

18 RH Farthing.............	8.00	10.00	12.00	18.00	65.00
19 RH Halfpenny, thick flan..	3.00	5.00	8.00	10.00	30.00
19a RH Halfpenny, thin flan...	5.00	7.00	10.00	15.00	45.00
20 RH Penny..............	7.00	10.00	15.00	20.00	50.00

21 Halfpenny, For General Accommodation........	2.00	3.00	5.00	7.00	15.00

The ship tokens, 22 through 25a, are lightweight tokens struck probably on Canadian order. The first is very rare, and has been denounced in the past as fraudulent. No evidence, however, has been found to establish this definitely. The reverse of 24 is that of a halfpenny token of Shaw, Jobson & Co. of Roscoe Mills, Sheffield, England, whose initials S. J. & Co. can be seen on the bale. The ship on this piece flies a pennant from the mainmast.

		V.G.	Fine	V.F.	E.F.	Unc.
22	Ship, no legends or date...	$35.00	$50.00	$70.00	$100.00	

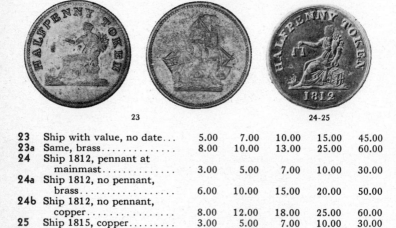

23   24-25

23	Ship with value, no date...	5.00	7.00	10.00	15.00	45.00
23a	Same, brass..............	8.00	10.00	13.00	25.00	60.00
24	Ship 1812, pennant at mainmast..............	3.00	5.00	7.00	10.00	30.00
24a	Ship 1812, no pennant, brass.................	6.00	10.00	15.00	20.00	50.00
24b	Ship 1812, no pennant, copper...............	8.00	12.00	18.00	25.00	60.00
25	Ship 1815, copper........	3.00	5.00	7.00	10.00	30.00
25a	Ship 1815, brass.........	6.00	10.00	15.00	20.00	50.00

The Anchor and H halfpennies are rather crudely made. It has been said that they were issued in Halifax, Nova Scotia, but this has not yet been proved.

26	Anchor and H, 1814......	75.00	125.00	200.00
27	Same, 1816..............	50.00	75.00	125.00

Doubtful Pieces

In view of the results of recent research, it is doubtful that these two pieces should continue to be listed among the Canadian colonial series. The BRITISH COLONIES tokens were originally sent to Jamaica and circulated as pennies. They were unacceptable there, and the shipment was later sent to Canada and put into circulation as halfpennies. Specimens have recently been found in Jamaica, which proved that the early English writers were right in assigning it to that colony. On the other hand, it has also been found in Canada, and therefore Canadian writers were not entirely wrong in listing it among the anonymous Canadian tokens.

The larger piece was issued for use in British Guiana in 1838, at a time when an oversupply of paper money was troublesome. Some specimens doubtless were brought to Canada, probably into Nova Scotia, but the date is too late for any piece specifically intended for a private issuer in Canada.

		V.G.	Fine	V.F.	E.F.	Unc.
28	British Colonies 1825......	$4.00	$7.00	$10.00	$15.00	$50.00

		V.G.	Fine	V.F.	E.F.	Unc.
29	Trade & Navigation 1838, thick flan.............	4.00	7.00	10.00	15.00	50.00
29a	Same, thin flan..........	4.00	7.00	10.00	15.00	50.00

5

NEWFOUNDLAND

Newfoundland was discovered by John Cabot in 1497 and claimed for England. The city of St. John's dates from about 1500. English authority was firmly established by Sir Humphrey Gilbert in 1583. Further settlements took place after 1600, but the French planted some colonies along the south coast at and near Placentia. These were ceded to the British in 1710.

Private Tokens 1815-1860
Magdalen Islands

This penny token was issued by Isaac Coffin, who planned to rule the islands like a feudal baron. At this time the islands were part of the colony of Newfoundland. Coffin soon learned that he did not have the powers of a colonial governor, but his pennies must have circulated for a long time, since they are rather rare in very fine or better condition. In 1825 the Magdalen Islands were transferred from the administration of Newfoundland to that of Lower Canada, which is now the province of Quebec.

		Good	V.G.	Fine	V.F.	E.F.
30	Penny token 1815........	$3.00	$6.00	$15.00	$25.00	$35.00

Rutherford Tokens

There was no coinage for Newfoundland until 1841, when the first copper tokens appeared. The Rutherford tokens were issued in 1841 and 1846, those of 1846 being struck by Ralph Heaton & Sons of Birmingham, England. These tokens became plentiful enough to become a nuisance, and they fell into discredit after 1850.

31-32 obv.　　　　　31 rev.　　　　　32 rev.

		V.G.	Fine	V.F.	E.F.	Unc.
31	No date, thick flan........	$1.50	$2.50	$5.00	$8.00	$25.00
31a	Same, thin flan..........	1.50	2.50	5.00	8.00	25.00
32	1841, thick flan..........	1.50	2.50	5.00	8.00	25.00
32a	1841, thin flan...........	1.50	2.50	5.00	8.00	25.00

33   33a   33b

33	1846, fine wool..........	1.75	2.75	6.00	10.00	27.50
33a	1846, coarse wool........	1.75	2.75	6.00	10.00	27.50
33b	1846, stars at sides	3.00	5.00	8.00	12.50	30.00

M'Auslane Token

Number 34, of farthing size, appeared about 1857. It was issued by Peter M'Auslane, a general merchant whose business at St. John's was destroyed by fire shortly afterward. He then quit the island and settled in Ontario.

34	M'Auslane farthing	200.00	250.00	350.00	450.00	—

Anonymous Issues

At this time lightweight halfpennies were being brought over by the barrel from Prince Edward Island, and in 1851 and again in 1860 the government had to forbid their further importation and use. The rare ship token of 1858 was struck by Heaton and issued at St. John's anonymously. It has been faked, but according to Breton, the fakes were easily exposed.

The "Fishery Rights" token of 1860 commemorates the signing of a treaty by the major fishing nations to regulate the fisheries. Shore limits were fixed, the rights of local fishermen were recognized, and steps were taken to control the behavior of foreign seamen whose vessels had to use local harbors for shelter or repairs.

		V.G.	Fine	V.F.	E.F.	Unc.
35	Ship 1858, thick flan	$125.00	$175.00	$225.00	$300.00	$400.00
35a	Ship 1858, thin flan	125.00	175.00	225.00	300.00	400.00
36	Fishery Rights 1860	15.00	20.00	25.00	35.00	60.00

DECIMAL COINAGE 1865-1947

In an act of 1863 Newfoundland turned to decimal currency, adopting the Spanish dollar as the unit. This made the English shilling equivalent to 24 cents and the sixpence to 12 cents.

1 CENT
Victoria Coinage 1865-1896

The obverse, designed and engraved by L. C. Wyon, is unusual in two respects. First, the portrait was one of those used for the English halfpence (from Peck's obv. 6), and second, the lettering is in simple, very bold type.

The reverse was engraved by Wyon's assistant, T. J. Minton, from a design by Horace Morehen. The wreath consists of pitcher plant (see pg. 82) and oak.

1880 date varieties. Two styles of the 0, narrow and wide, are known. The position of the wide 0 also varies; however, these positional differences are considered trivial and will not be perpetuated here.

Diameter: 25.53 mm; weight: 5.670 grams; composition: .950 copper, .040 tin, .010 zinc; edge: plain.

G. — *Hair over ear worn through.*

V.G. — *Little detail to hair over the ear or the braid.*

Fine — *Strands of hair over ear begin to merge, braid is worn.*

V.F. — *Hair over ear is worn, braid is clear but no longer sharp.*

E.F. — *Slight wear on hair over ear, braid that holds knot in place is sharp and clear.*

Date	Approx. Minted	Good	V.G.	Fine	V.F.	E.F.	Toned Unc.	Brill. Unc.
1865	240,000	$ .50	$1.00	$2.00	$3.50	$6.00	$30.00	$60.00
1872H	200,000	.50	1.00	2.00	3.50	6.00	30.00	55.00
1873	200,025	.50	1.00	2.00	3.50	6.00	35.00	60.00
1876H	200,000	.50	1.00	2.00	3.50	6.00	30.00	55.00

		Narrow 0			Wide 0			
Date	Approx. Minted	Good	V.G.	Fine	V.F.	E.F.	Toned Unc.	Brill. Unc.
1880								
nar. 0.	} 400,000	$20.00	$30.00	$45.00	$80.00	$100.00	$175.00	$300.00
wide 0.		.50	1.00	2.00	3.50	6.00	35.00	60.00
1885 40,000		5.00	9.00	17.50	22.50	27.50	75.00	160.00
1888 50,000		4.00	8.00	15.00	20.00	25.00	55.00	135.00
1890 200,000		.40	.90	1.75	3.25	5.50	20.00	45.00
1894 200,000		.40	.90	1.75	3.25	5.50	20.00	45.00
1896 200,000		.40	.90	1.75	3.25	5.50	20.00	45.00

Edward VII Coinage 1904-1909

The obverse was derived from a portrait model by G. W. De Saulles; the portrait is unusually large for the size of the coin.

The reverse design is the same as that for the Victoria series, except for the substitution of the Imperial State crown for the St. Edward's crown. The modification was made by W. H. J. Blakemore.

Diameter: 25.53 mm; weight: 5.670 grams; composition: .950 copper, .040 tin, .010 zinc; edge: plain.

G. — Band of crown worn through.

V.G. — Band of the crown is worn through at the highest point.

Fine — Jewels in the band of crown will be blurred.

V.F. — Band of the crown is still clear but no longer sharp.

E.F. — Band of the crown slightly worn but generally sharp and clear.

1904H . . . 100,000	2.00	4.00	6.50	12.00	17.50	40.00	100.00
1907 200,000	.50	1.00	2.00	3.50	7.00	25.00	50.00
1909 200,000	.50	1.00	2.00	3.50	7.00	25.00	50.00

George V Coinage 1913-1936

The obverse, from a portrait model by Sir E. B. MacKennal (B. M. on truncation), is identical to that for the Canadian issues of the same denomination.

The reverse is a continuation of the design introduced in the Edward VII series.

Diameter 1913, 1929, 1936: 25.53 mm; 1917-20: 25.40 mm; weight: 5.670 grams; composition 1913-20: .950 copper, .040 tin, .010 zinc; 1929-36: .955 copper, .030 tin, .015 zinc; edge: plain.

G. — Band of crown worn through.

V.G. — Band of the crown is worn through at the highest point.

Fine — Jewels in the band of crown will be blurred.

V.F. — Band of the crown is still clear but no longer sharp.

E.F. — Band of the crown slightly worn but generally sharp and clear.

Date	Quan. Minted	Good	V.G.	Fine	V.F.	E.F.	Toned Unc.	Brill. Unc.
1913....400,000		$ .25	$ .50	$1.00	$1.75	$3.00	$15.00	$35.00
1917C...702,350		.20	.40	.85	1.50	2.75	12.00	21.50
1919C...300,000		.25	.50	1.00	1.75	3.00	12.00	21.50
1920C...302,184		.25	.50	1.00	1.75	3.00	12.00	21.50
1929....300,000		.20	.40	.85	1.50	2.75	12.00	21.50
1936....300,000		.20	.35	.70	1.25	2.00	10.00	19.00

George VI Coinage 1938-1947

The obverse is derived from a portrait model by Percy Metcalfe (P.M. below neck) intended for English colonial coinages.

The reverse device is the pitcher plant, *Sarracenia purpurea*, which is native to the island of Newfoundland. This interesting plant is insectivorous, each leaf forming a receptacle at the bottom of which is a liquid that induces the prey to enter the leaf. Spines lining the inner leaf surface help prevent the insect from leaving after it has entered. Once in the sticky liquid, the insect is digested and absorbed by the plant. The designer is unknown.

Diameter: 19.05 mm; weight: 3.240 grams; composition: .955 copper, .030 tin, .015 zinc; edge: plain.

V.G. — *Band of crown almost worn through. Little detail in hair.*
Fine — *Band of crown considerably worn, strands of hair begin to merge together.*
V.F. — *Wear extends along band of crown, hair is clear but no longer sharp.*
E.F. — *Band of crown shows slight wear, hair is sharp and clear.*

Date	Quan. Minted	V.G.	Fine	V.F.	E.F.	Toned Unc.	Brill. Unc.
1938...........500,000		.50	.75	1.25	2.25	6.50	12.50
1940...........300,000		2.25	3.25	4.50	6.50	15.00	30.00
1941C.........827,662		.25	.40	.50	.85	4.50	8.00
1942.........1,996,889		.25	.40	.50	.85	4.50	8.00
1943C.........1,239,732		.25	.40	.50	.85	4.50	8.00
1944C.........1,328,776		1.00	1.50	2.25	3.50	12.50	22.50
1947C.........313,772		.50	.75	1.25	2.25	6.00	12.00

5 CENTS

Victoria Coinage 1865-1896

The initial obverse was derived from that for New Brunswick by the appropriate modification of the legend. Periods are present on both sides of NEWFOUNDLAND. A second variety lacks the periods. On the final obverse the Queen has more aged facial features with repressed upper lip and recessed forehead, and the period after NEWFOUNDLAND was restored (closer to the D, however).

Two noteworthy reverses are known for this series. The first has a Roman I in the date, while the second has the more conventional Arabic 1.

The first and probably all later obverse and reverse varieties were designed and engraved by L. C. Wyon.

The weights of the silver denominations were made proportional to those of the equivalent values in English silver coin; that is, 5.6552 grams per shilling (12 pence). The value of the 5 cents was 2½d.

Diameter: 15.49 mm; weight: 1.178 grams; composition: .925 silver, .075 copper; edge: reeded.

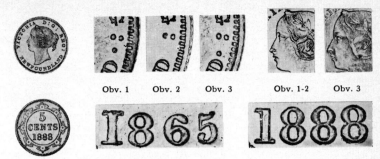

Obv. 1   Obv. 2   Obv. 3   Obv. 1-2   Obv. 3

Roman I   Arabic 1

G. — Braid near ear worn through.
V.G. — No details in braid around the ear.
Fine — Segments of braid begin to merge into one
    another.
V.F. — Braid is clear but not sharp.
E.F. — Braid is slightly worn but generally sharp
    and clear.

Roman I Reverse (1865)

Date	Obverse No.	Approx. Minted	Good	V.G.	Fine	V.F.	E.F.	Unc.
1865	1, 2	80,000	$8.00	$12.00	$17.50	$25.00	$37.50	$100.00

Arabic 1 Reverse (1870-1896)

Date	Obverse No.	Approx. Minted	Good	V.G.	Fine	V.F.	E.F.	Unc.
1870	1, 2	40,000	9.00	14.00	20.00	27.50	40.00	110.00
1872H	2	40,000	8.00	12.00	17.50	25.00	37.50	100.00
1873	2	} 44,260	9.00	14.00	20.00	27.50	40.00	110.00
1873H	2		100.00	150.00	225.00	350.00	500.00	900.00
1876H	2	20,000	15.00	22.50	30.00	45.00	70.00	225.00
1880	2	40,000	8.00	12.00	17.50	30.00	50.00	175.00
1881	2	40,000	7.00	10.00	15.00	20.00	37.50	75.00
1882H	3	60,000	6.00	8.00	12.00	17.50	27.50	70.00
1885	2	16,000	35.00	50.00	65.00	90.00	175.00	425.00
1888	2, 3	40,000	6.00	8.00	12.00	17.50	27.50	70.00
1890	3	160,000		2.50	5.00	9.00	17.50	60.00
1894	3	160,000		2.50	5.00	9.00	17.50	60.00
1896	3	400,000		2.00	4.50	8.00	15.00	55.00

Edward VII Coinage 1903-1908

The obverse, designed and engraved by G. W. De Saulles (DES. below bust), is identical to that for the Canadian issues.

The reverse was designed by W. H. J. Blakemore.

Diameter: 15.49 mm; weight: 1.178 grams; composition: .925 silver, .075 copper; edge: reeded.

G. — Band of crown worn through.
V.G. — Band of the crown is worn through at the
    highest point.
Fine — Jewels in the band of crown will be blurred.
V.F.— Band of crown still clear but no longer sharp.
E.F. — Band of the crown slightly worn but gener-
    ally sharp and clear.

Date	Approx. Minted	Good	V.G.	Fine	V.F.	E.F.	Unc.
1903	100,000	$1.00	$2.00	$3.50	$6.00	$15.00	$65.00
1904H	100,000	1.00	2.00	3.50	6.00	15.00	65.00
1908	400,000	.75	1.75	2.75	4.50	12.00	55.00

George V Coinage 1912-1929

The obverse bears a portrait derived from a model by Sir E. B. MacKennal (B.M. on truncation) and is identical to that for the Canadian issues.
The reverse is as for the Edward VII series.

Diameter 1912-19: 15.49 mm; 1929: 15.69 mm; weight 1912: 1.178 grams; 1917-29: 1.166 grams; composition: .925 silver, .075 copper; edge: reeded.

G. — Band of crown worn through.
V.G — Band of the crown is worn through at the highest point.
Fine — Jewels in the band of crown will be blurred.
V.F.— Band of crown still clear but no longer sharp.
E.F. — Band of the crown slightly worn but generally sharp and clear.

Date	Quan. Minted	V.G.	Fine	V.F.	E.F.	Unc.
1912	300,000	$ .80	$1.35	$2.75	$6.00	$25.00
1917C	300,319	.80	1.35	2.75	6.00	25.00
1919C	100,844	1.10	2.25	4.50	9.00	37.50
1929	300,000	.50	.90	1.60	4.00	22.50

George VI Coinage 1938-1947

The obverse is derived from a portrait model by Percy Metcalfe (P.M. below neck) intended for English colonial coinages.
The reverse is as for the Edward VII and George V issues.

Diameter 1938: 15.69 mm; 1940-47: 15.49 mm; weight: 1.166 grams; composition 1938-44: .925 silver, .075 copper; 1945-47: .800 silver, .200 copper, edge: reeded.

V.G. — The band is almost worn through. Little detail of the hair.
Fine — The band of the crown is considerably worn and the strands of hair begin to merge together.
V.F. — Wear extends along the band of the crown and the hair is clear but no longer sharp.
E.F. — Band of the crown shows slight wear and the hair is sharp and clear.

1938	100,000	.50	.75	1.50	3.00	12.00
1940C	200,000	.40	.60	.90	1.75	6.50
1941C	612,641	.25	.40	.60	1.00	5.50
1942C	298,348	1.00	1.50	2.25	3.00	9.00
1943C	351,666	.20	.35	.50	.90	5.00
1944C	286,504	.50	.75	1.50	2.25	7.50
1945C	203,828	.20	.35	.50	.90	4.50
1946C	2,041	90.00	120.00	140.00	175.00	225.00
1947C	38,400	3.00	5.00	7.50	10.00	21.00

10 CENTS
Victoria Coinage 1865-1896

The portrait on the initial obverse was derived from and is almost identical to Wyon's Canadian portrait 6 for the same denomination. A second obverse is the same except it lacks the period after NEWFOUNDLAND. The final variety, derived from the first, has the period after NEWFOUNDLAND and a Queen with more aged facial features. Two noteworthy reverses are known for this series. The first has Roman I's in the I0 and date, while the second has the more conventional Arabic 1's. There are also slight differences in the devices and rim denticles.

The weights of the silver denominations were made proportional to those of the equivalent values in English silver coin; that is, 5.6552 grams per shilling (12 pence). The value of the 10 cents was 5d.

1880 2nd 8 over 7. All of the 10 and 50 cents of 1880 examined have the second 8 in the date punched over a 7. By the latter part of the 1870's, the dies for these denominations were sunk from reverse punches bearing the partial date 187-; the final digit was hand punched into each die. In 1880, then, the Mint was faced with either making new punches or using the old ones and correcting the 7 in each die, in addition to adding the final digit. The latter course of action was chosen in 1880, probably because of a lack of time and the small number of dies which had to be made for Newfoundland in that year. The reverse punches for the other denominations lacked both the third and the fourth digits, so this problem did not arise for them.

Diameter: 17.96 mm; weight: 2.356 grams; composition; .925 silver, .025 copper; edge: reeded.

| | Obv. 1-2 | Obv. 3 | | Obv. 1 | Obv. 2 | Obv. 3 |

Roman I   Arabic 1 (note 2nd 8 over 7)

G. — *Braid around ear worn through.*
V.G. — *No details in braid around the ear.*
Fine — *Segments of braid begin to merge into one another.*
V.F. — *Braid is clear but not sharp.*
E.F. — *Braid is slightly worn but generally sharp and clear.*

Date	Obverse No.	Approx. Minted	Good	V.G.	Fine	V.F.	E.F.	Unc.
Roman I's Reverse (1865-70)								
1865	1	80,000	$4.00	$7.50	$12.50	$20.00	$30.00	$110.00
1870	1, 2	30,000	60.00	100.00	150.00	200.00	300.00	550.00
Arabic I's Reverse (1872-96)								
1872H	2	40,000	3.00	5.50	9.00	13.50	25.00	100.00
1873	1, 2	23,614	4.00	7.50	12.50	20.00	30.00	110.00
1876H	2	10,000	12.50	17.50	22.50	30.00	75.00	225.00
1880, 2nd 8 over 7	2	10,000	12.50	17.50	22.50	30.00	75.00	225.00
1882H	3	20,000	3.00	5.50	9.00	13.50	22.50	95.00
1885	2	8,000	22.50	30.00	45.00	67.50	150.00	300.00
1888	3	30,000	2.50	5.00	8.50	13.50	25.00	100.00
1890H	3	100,000	1.25	2.50	5.00	9.00	20.00	65.00
1894	2, 3	100,000	1.25	2.50	5.00	9.00	20.00	65.00
1896	3	230,000	1.00	2.00	4.00	7.50	15.00	60.00

Edward VII Coinage 1903-1904

The obverse, designed and engraved by **G. W. De Saulles** (DES. below bust), is identical to that for the Canadian issues.

The reverse was designed by W. H. J. Blakemore.

Diameter: 17.96 mm; weight: 2.356 grams; composition: .925 silver, .025 copper; edge: reeded.

G. — *Band of crown worn through.*
V.G. — *Band of the crown is worn through at the highest point.*
Fine — *Jewels in band of crown will be blurred.*
V.F. — *Band of the crown is still clear but no longer sharp.*
E.F. — *Band of the crown slightly worn but generally sharp and clear.*

Date	Quan. Minted	Good	V.G.	Fine	V.F.	E.F.	Unc.
1903	100,000	$1.50	$2.00	$4.00	$8.00	$25.00	$85.00
1904H	100,000	1.00	1.50	3.50	7.50	22.50	80.00

George V Coinage 1912-1919

The obverse bears a portrait derived from a model by Sir E. B. MacKennal (B.M. on truncation) and is identical to that for the Canadian issues.
The reverse is identical to that of the Edward VII series.

Diameter 1912: 17.96 mm; 1917, 1919: 18.03 mm; weight 1912: 2.356 grams; 1917, 1919: 2.333 grams; composition: .925 silver, .075 copper; edge: reeded.

G. — *Band of crown worn through.*
V.G. — *Band of the crown is worn through at the highest point.*
Fine — *Jewels in band of crown will be blurred.*
V.F. — *Band of the crown is still clear but no longer sharp.*
E.F. — *Band of the crown slightly worn but generally sharp and clear.*

1912	150,000	1.25	2.00	3.00	6.50	15.00	55.00
1917C	250,805	.75	1.25	2.00	4.00	10.00	55.00
1919C	54,342	1.50	2.50	4.50	8.00	20.00	60.00

George VI Coinage 1938-1947

The obverse is derived from a portrait model by Percy Metcalfe (P.M. below neck) intended for English colonial coinages.
The reverse is as for the Edward VII and George V issues.

Diameter: 18.03 mm; weight: 2.333 grams; composition 1938-44: .925 silver, .075 copper; 1945-47: .800 silver, .200 copper; edge: reeded.

V.G. — *The band is almost worn through. Little detail of the hair.*
Fine — *Band of crown is considerably worn and the strands of hair begin to merge together.*
V.F. — *Wear extends along band of crown and the hair is clear but no longer sharp.*
E.F. — *Band of the crown shows slight wear and the hair is sharp and clear.*

Date	Quan. Minted	V.G.	Fine	V.F.	E.F.	Unc.
1938	100,000	.40	.75	1.50	3.50	12.50
1940	100,000	.40	.75	1.50	3.00	11.00
1941C	483,630	.35	.50	.90	2.00	10.00
1942C	292,736	.35	.50	.90	2.00	10.00
1943C	104,706	.35	.50	.90	2.00	10.00
1944C	151,471	.40	.75	1.50	3.00	10.00
1945C	175,833	.35	.50	.90	2.00	10.00
1946C	38,400	3.25	5.00	7.50	10.00	30.00
1947C	61,988	1.25	2.50	3.75	5.50	17.50

20 CENTS
Victoria Coinage 1865-1900

The portrait on the initial obverse was derived from and is almost identical to Wyon's Canadian portrait for the same denomination. A second obverse, which was derived from the first, has the Queen with more aged facial features: slightly double chin, repressed upper lip and recessed forehead.

The reverses for the 1865 to 1881 issues have a Roman I in the date; later issues have the more conventional Arabic 1 in the date.

The weights of the silver denominations were made proportional to those of the equivalent values in English silver coin; that is, 5.6552 grams per shilling (12 pence). The value of the 20 cents was 10d.

Diameter: 23.19 mm; weight: 4.713 grams; composition: .925 silver, .075 copper; edge: reeded.

Obv. 1   Obv. 2   Roman I   Arabic 1

G. — *Braid around ear worn through.*
V.G. — *No details in braid around the ear.*
Fine — *Segments of braid begin to merge into one another.*
V.F. — *Braid is clear but not sharp.*
E.F. — *Braid is slightly worn but generally sharp and clear.*

Date	Portrait No.	Approx. Minted	Good	V.G.	Fine	V.F.	E.F.	Unc.
Roman I Reverse (1865-1881)								
1865	1	100,000	$1.50	$3.00	$7.00	$14.00	$30.00	$110.00
1870	1	50,000	2.50	5.00	8.00	17.50	40.00	135.00
1872H	1	90,000	1.50	3.00	7.00	14.00	30.00	110.00
1873	1	45,799	1.50	3.00	7.00	14.00	32.50	120.00
1876H	1	50,000	2.50	5.00	8.00	17.50	40.00	135.00
1880	1	30,000	2.50	5.00	8.00	17.50	40.00	135.00
1881	1	60,000	.75	1.50	2.50	5.00	17.50	75.00
Arabic 1 Reverse (1882-1900)								
1882H	2	100,000	.60	1.00	2.00	4.00	15.00	70.00
1885	1	40,000	1.00	1.75	3.00	6.00	20.00	80.00
1888	2	75,000	.60	1.00	2.00	3.50	12.50	65.00
1890	2	100,000	.50	.90	1.50	3.00	10.00	60.00
1894	1	100,000	.50	.90	1.50	3.00	10.00	60.00
1896 sm. 96	2	} 125,000	.50	.90	1.50	3.00	10.00	60.00
lg. 96	2		.60	1.00	2.00	3.50	12.50	65.00
1899 sm. 99	2	} 125,000	.60	1.00	2.00	3.50	12.50	65.00
lg. 99	2		.45	.85	1.25	2.75	9.00	50.00
1900	2	125,000	.45	.85	1.25	2.75	9.00	50.00

Edward VII Coinage 1904

The obverse was derived from a portrait model by G. W. De Saulles (DES. below bust).

The reverse was designed and engraved by W. H. J. Blakemore.

Diameter: 23.19 mm; weight: 4.713 grams; composition: .925 silver, .075 copper; edge: reeded.

G. — *Band of crown worn through.*
V.G. — *Band of the crown is worn through at the highest point.*
Fine — *Jewels in the band of crown will be blurred.*
V.F. — *Band of the crown is still clear but no longer sharp.*
E.F. — *Band of the crown slightly worn but generally sharp and clear.*

Date	Approx. Minted	Good	V.G.	Fine	V.F.	E.F.	Unc.
1904H	75,000	$2.50	$4.00	$7.00	$10.00	$25.00	$125.00

George V Coinage 1912

The obverse was derived from a portrait model of the King by Sir E. B. MacKennal (B.M. on truncation).

The reverse was a continuation of the design introduced in the Edward VII series.

Diameter: 23.19 mm; weight: 4.713 grams; composition: .925 silver, .075 copper; edge: reeded.

G. — *Band of crown worn through.*
V.G. — *Band of crown worn through at highest point.*
Fine — *Jewels in band of crown will be blurred.*
V.F. — *Band of crown still clear but no longer sharp.*
E.F. — *Band of crown slightly worn but generally sharp and clear.*

Date	Minted	Good	V.G.	Fine	V.F.	E.F.	Unc.
1912	350,000	.50	.75	1.25	2.75	7.50	37.50

25 CENTS

George V Coinage 1917-1919

Because of continuing difficulties arising from confusion of Canadian 25 and Newfoundland 20 cent pieces, the latter denomination was discontinued and a 25 cent coin struck instead.

The obverse, from a portrait model by Sir E. B. MacKennal (B.M. on truncation), is identical to that for the Canadian issues of the same denomination.

W. H. J. Blakemore designed and engraved the reverse.

Date	Quan. Minted	Good	V.G.	Fine	V.F.	E.F.	Unc.
1917C	464,779	$ .50	$ .60	$ .90	$1.25	$2.75	$15.00
1919C	163,939	.60	.75	1.20	1.50	3.50	20.00

50 CENTS
Victoria Coinage 1870-1900

This denomination has a laureate bust which thereby distinctly differs from that on the Canadian 50 cents. There are two portrait varieties; the first has a "youthful" prominent upper lip, while the second, derived from the first, has an "aged" repressed lip.

The initial reverse is characterized by the presence of a small date and thick loops near the rim denticles. A second design has a larger date and thin loops.

L. C. Wyon was the designer and engraver of the first and probably the later designs as well.

The weights of the silver denominations were made proportional to those of the equivalent values in English silver coin; that is, 5.6552 grams per shilling (12 pence). The value of the 50 cents was 2s. 1d.

1880 2nd 8 over 7. See page 85 for details.

Diameter: 29.85 mm; weight: 11.782 grams; composition: .925 silver, .075 copper; edge: eeded.

Obv. 1   Obv. 2

Thick loops, small
date (above)
Thin loops, large
date (below)

G. — *Braid around ear worn through.*

V.G. — *No details in braid around the ear.*

Fine — *Segments of braid begin to merge into one another.*

V.F. — *Braid is clear but not sharp.*

E.F. — *Braid is slightly worn but generally sharp and clear.*

Date	Portrait No.	Approx. Minted	Good	V.G.	Fine	V.F.	E.F.	Unc.
Thick Loops Reverse (1870-1881)								
1870	1	50,000	$1.50	$3.00	$6.00	$10.00	$25.00	$175.00
1872H	1	48,000	1.50	3.00	6.00	10.00	25.00	175.00
1873	1	37,675	1.50	3.00	6.00	10.00	25.00	175.00
1874	1	80,000	1.50	3.00	6.00	10.00	25.00	175.00
1876H	1	28,000	3.00	6.00	11.00	17.50	37.50	240.00
1880, 2nd 8 over 7	1	24,000	3.00	6.00	11.00	17.50	37.50	240.00
1881	1	50,000	2.00	4.00	7.50	12.50	27.50	185.00
Thin Loops Reverse (1882-1900)								
1882H	2	100,000	1.25	2.50	5.00	9.00	20.00	175.00
1885	1	40,000	1.50	3.00	6.00	10.00	20.00	175.00
1888	1	20,000	2.00	4.00	7.00	12.50	35.00	180.00
1894	1	40,000	1.00	1.75	3.00	5.00	17.50	140.00
1896	1	60,000	1.00	1.75	3.00	5.00	17.50	140.00
1898	2	76,607	.90	1.50	2.50	4.00	12.50	140.00

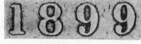

Narrow 9's   Wide 9's

Date	Portrait No.	Approx. Minted	Good	V.G.	Fine	V.F.	E.F.	Unc.
1899 narrow 9's	2	} 150,000	.90	1.50	2.50	4.00	12.50	140.00
wide 9's	2		.90	1.50	2.50	4.00	12.50	140.00
1900	2	150,000	.75	.90	1.75	3.00	10.00	125.00

Edward VII Coinage 1904-1909

The obverse, designed and engraved by G. W. De Saulles (DES below bust), is identical to that for the Canadian issues.

The reverse was designed by W. H. J. Blakemore.

Diameter: 29.85 mm; weight: 11.782 grams; composition: .925 silver, .075 copper; edge: reeded.

G. — *Band of crown is worn through.*

V.G. — *Band of the crown is worn through at the highest point.*

Fine — *Jewels in the band of crown will be blurred.*

V.F. — *Band of the crown is still clear but no longer sharp.*

E.F. — *Band of the crown slightly worn but generally sharp and clear.*

Date	Quan. Minted	Good	V.G.	Fine	V.F.	E.F.	Unc.
1904H	140,000	$ .85	$1.00	$1.50	$4.00	$7.50	$60.00
1907	100,000	.90	1.25	2.00	5.00	10.00	65.00
1908	160,000	.85	1.00	1.50	4.00	7.50	55.00
1909	200,000	.85	1.00	1.50	4.00	7.50	55.00

George V Coinage 1911-1919

The obverse was derived from a portrait model by Sir E. B. MacKennal (B.M. on truncation) and is identical to that used for the 1912-36 Canadian issues. It should be noted that the legend contains DEI GRA: ("by the Grace of God"), a feature which was absent on the 1911 Canadian issue of the same denomination.

The reverse is as for the Edward VII series.

Diameter 1911: 29.85 mm; 1917-19: 29.72 mm; weight 1911: 11.782 grams; 1917-19: 11.664 grams; composition: .925 silver, .075 copper; edge: reeded.

G. — Band of crown is worn through.

V.G. — Band of the crown is worn through at the highest point.

Fine — Jewels in the band of crown will be blurred.

V.F. — Band of the crown is still clear but no longer sharp.

E.F. — Band of the crown slightly worn but generally sharp and clear.

Date	Quan. Minted	Good	V.G.	Fine	V.F.	E.F.	Unc.
1911............	200,000	$ .75	$1.00	$1.50	$3.00	$7.50	$35.00
1917C.........	375,560	.75	1.00	1.50	3.00	7.50	35.00
1918C.........	294,824	.75	1.00	1.50	3.00	7.50	35.00
1919C.........	306,267	.75	1.00	1.50	3.00	7.50	35.00

GOLD 2 DOLLARS
Victoria Coinage 1865-1888

This interesting series of "double dollars," as they were sometimes called, gives Newfoundland the distinction of being the only English colony with its own issue of gold.

There are three obverse varieties.

Because this denomination is the same diameter as the 10 cents, the obverses in both cases were derived from the same matrices and punches (and perhaps dies). See page 84 for details on the three obverse varieties.

The reverse was designed and engraved by L. C. Wyon.

Diameter: 17.96 mm; weight: 3.328 grams; composition: .917 gold, .083 copper; edge: reeded.

Fine — Segments of braid begin to merge into one another.

V.F. — Braid is clear but not sharp.

E.F. — Braid is slightly worn but generally sharp and clear.

Date	Portrait No.	Approx. Minted	V.G.	Fine	V.F.	E.F.	Unc.
1865...............	1	10,000	32.50	42.50	55.00	70.00	92.50
1870...............	1, 2	10,000	32.50	42.50	55.00	70.00	92.50
1872...............	2	6,050	50.00	75.00	100.00	120.00	160.00
1880...............	2	2,500	100.00	200.00	300.00	400.00	500.00
1881...............	2	10,000	35.00	40.00	47.50	55.00	75.00
1882H............	3	25,000	30.00	35.00	40.00	45.00	60.00
1885...............	2	10,000	35.00	40.00	47.50	55.00	77.50
1888...............	2, 3	25,000	30.00	35.00	40.00	45.00	60.00

6

PRINCE EDWARD ISLAND

Prince Edward Island was colonized by France and originally named Isle St. Jean. It was acquired by Great Britain in 1758 and governed from Nova Scotia until 1770, when it was given the status of a separate colony. In 1794 it was given its present name in honor of Edward, Duke of Kent, the father of Queen Victoria.

The "Holey Dollar" of 1813

In 1813 the governor of Prince Edward Island ordered that a thousand Spanish dollars be perforated in the center, the rings to pass for five shillings and the centers, or "dumps," for one shilling. The resulting "holey dollars" and dumps were countermarked with the Treasury mark, a small circle bordered by ten triangles, resembling a rayed sun. On the rings the mark is seen partly on the Spanish king's forehead, ahead of the D in DEI. On the plugs it is partly on the throat.

These pieces were issued to supply the island with a silver currency that would not be exported, but they were withdrawn in 1814 on account of forgeries. The merchants then agreed to accept the forgeries in trade, thus raising them to the status of tokens. For this reason the counterfeits are called "merchants' forgeries" by collectors.

The mark on a genuine holey dollar has ten small triangles regularly spaced and of equal size. Merchants' forgeries bear marks somewhat less regular in dimensions. Some merchants' forgeries bear circles with ten triangles, and others have circles with eleven. Fakes have been made to deceive collectors. On these the mark is very crude, and occasionally in the wrong place.

		V.G.	Fine	V.F.	E.F.
37	Holey dollar, original..............	$800.00	$1,200	$1,500	$2,000
38	Dump, original..................		Extremely rare		
37a	Holey dollar, merchants' forgery...	500.00	700.00	1,000	1,500
38a	Dump, merchants' forgery.........	700.00	1,000	1,200	1,800

Ships Colonies & Commerce Tokens

The inscription on these pieces is an allusion to a remark made by Napoleon at the battle of Ulm. Ships, colonies, and commerce, he said, were the three British advantages that would defeat him in the end. The first tokens came out about 1829. These were struck in New York by Wright & Bale, and bear a striped flag superficially resembling the United States flag. These pieces were popular, and later issues were imported from England. Most were designed by Thomas Halliday. The two brass pieces dated 1815 were struck after 1830, being antedated to evade laws against anonymous tokens. The reverse of 40 is that of a private token of the Isle of Man.

	V.G.	Fine	V.F.	E.F.	Unc.
39 One Halfpenny Token 1815	$3.00	$5.00	$8.00	$12.00	—
40 For Publick Accommo- dation 1815............	3.00	5.00	8.00	12.00	—

41   41a

41 Ship with U.S. flag........	3.00	5.00	8.00	12.00	30.00
41a Same with W. & B.N.Y. ...	6.00	10.00	15.00	25.00	50.00

It is doubtful if 42, Breton's No. 999, will ever be positively identified. Its obverse, as drawn by Breton, shows a small ship very much like that of such Nova Scotia tokens as the Starr & Shannon pieces. Its reverse die has yet to be identified. The curved hull varieties (43, 43a) have been said to be Breton 999, but this is not so. Judge Lees, who published these pieces in *The Numismatist* in 1926, made this point very clear.

42 Small ship..............		Existence doubted			
43 Curved hull, thick flan....	—	—	—	—	—
43a Curved hull, thin flan.....	—	—	—	—	—

The next three varieties bear the same reverse, characterized by very large, bold lettering. The first, Breton 1000, is very rare. It has been called fraudulent, but without apparent proof.

		V.G.	Fine	V.F.	E.F.	Unc.
44	Long, low hull, no poopdeck	$75.00	$90.00	$125.00	$200.00	—

44a ← 44b →

44a	Short, choppy waves......	4.00	6.00	10.00	15.00	30.00
44b	Long, running waves......	3.00	5.00	8.00	12.50	25.00

The token numbered 997 by Breton has over forty minor die varieties, some of which are very rare. They were struck in Birmingham and designed by Thomas Halliday. Most of the varieties are in the reverse inscription. For example, four styles of "&" are found on varieties of 45, 45b and 45c. The varieties of 45a all have the "&" ending in a short horizontal bar.

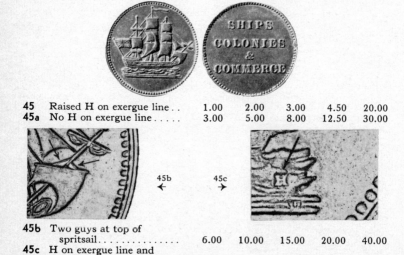

45	Raised H on exergue line..	1.00	2.00	3.00	4.50	20.00
45a	No H on exergue line.....	3.00	5.00	8.00	12.50	30.00

45b ← 45c →

45b	Two guys at top of spritsail..............	6.00	10.00	15.00	20.00	40.00
45c	H on exergue line and in water..............	2.00	3.50	6.00	10.00	25.00

Local Tokens 1840-1858

Local tokens appeared first in 1840, the rarest being the sheaf of wheat half-penny. It was struck by James Milner of Charlottetown with dies and machinery imported from the United States. The "Success to the Fisheries" tokens (47 to 47c) were issued by E. Lydiard and F. Longworth of Charlottetown. Those with a clevis to the plow were issued in 1840, and those with a hook in 1857. The large tail to the fish fillet is well struck up, while the small tail is weak. These and all later tokens were struck by Ralph Heaton & Sons.

		V.G.	Fine	V.F.	E.F.	Unc.
46	Sheaf of Wheat 1840......	$50.00	$75.00	$100.00	—	—

Clevis　　　　Hook

Small Tail　　　Large Tail

47	Clevis, small tail..........	1.50	2.50	5.00	8.00	15.00
47a	Clevis, large tail..........	3.00	5.00	8.00	12.50	25.00
47c	Hook, small tail..........	3.00	5.00	8.00	12.50	25.00
47d	Hook, large tail..........	1.50	2.50	5.00	8.00	15.00

The "Cent" of 1855 was issued by James Duncan, a hardware merchant who moved to Charlottetown from Montreal. This is the first Canadian decimal piece. It is doubtful if it was accepted as a hundredth of a dollar, for it weighed the same as the other tokens which were halfpennies and which went at 150 to the Spanish dollar. Specimens on thicker flans may have been an attempt to pass them as cents by increasing the weight.

The token showing the paddle steamer was issued in 1858, probably by James Duncan, though this has not been established. Early writers attributed it to Newfoundland.

		V.G.	Fine	V.F.	E.F.	Unc.
48	1 Cent 1855, thin flan.....	$1.50	$3.00	$5.00	$8.00	$20.00
48a	Same, thick flan..........	2.00	4.00	7.00	10.00	25.00
49	Paddle steamer, thick flan .	2.50	4.00	6.00	10.00	25.00
49a	Paddle steamer, thin flan ..	3.50	5.00	7.50	12.50	35.00

The tokens inscribed "Self Government and Free Trade" were issued by Henry Haszard and George and Simeon Davies. There are thirty minor varieties in all — four each of 50 and 50a and twenty-two of 51.

50	Prince Edward's Is. 1855 ..	1.50	3.00	5.00	8.00	20.00
50a	Prince Edward Is. 1855....	1.50	3.00	5.00	8.00	20.00
51	Prince Edward Is. 1857....	1.00	2.00	3.00	6.00	15.00

Decimal Issue 1871

In 1871 the island adopted a decimal system, based on the same unit (the U.S. gold dollar) as that of Canada. Only the 1 cent denomination was issued prior to its entry into the Confederation in 1873.

1 CENT

The obverse was designed and engraved by L. C. Wyon, based on a portrait model by William Theed, and is identical to that for the Jamaica halfpenny of the same year.

The reverse was adapted by L. C. Wyon from the Government seal of the island. The device is composed of a large oak tree (representing England) sheltering three oak saplings (representing the three counties of the island); beneath these is the Latin phrase *Parva Sub Ingenti,* meaning "The small beneath the great."

The issue is distinctive in that it was struck at the Heaton Mint in Birmingham, but lacks the familiar H mint mark and has English titles rather than Latin on the obverse.

Diameter: 25.40 mm; weight: 5.670 grams; composition: .950 copper, .040 tin, .010 zinc; edge: plain.

G. — *Hair over ear worn through.*
V.G. — *No details in hair over ear.*
Fine — *Strands of hair over ear begin to run together.*
V.F. — *Hair and jewels no longer sharp, but clear.*
E.F. — *Hair over ear sharp and clear. Jewels in diadem must show sharply and clearly.*

Date	Quan. Minted	Good	V.G.	Fine	V.F.	E.F.	Toned Unc.	Brill. Unc.
1871...	2,000,000	.40	.70	1.00	1.50	2.50	25.00	95.00

NOVA SCOTIA

Nova Scotia was colonized for the first time in 1604 by Sieur de Monts, who claimed the land for France under the name of Acadia. Captured several times by the English, it was always returned to France, but in 1713 it passed permanently into English hands and renamed Nova Scotia.

Very little coined money was available in the early days under the English. Some Spanish dollars and occasional shipments of English halfpennies and farthings were almost the only coins to be had. The Spanish dollar was accepted in Halifax at five shillings, which rating became legal by 1758. Halifax Currency, as this rating was called, was destined to become the standard of all the Canadian colonies.

Trade & Navigation Tokens 1812-14

After 1800 the shortage of copper began to become serious, and about 1812 local merchants started to import tokens from England and Ireland. The first were the "Trade & Navigation" tokens, struck over the tokens of Samuel Guppy of Bristol. The farthing is known to have been imported by a Halifax merchant named Haliburton.

For many years there have been reports of a penny bearing the date 1812, but in recent years none has been found. Early auction sales record specimens dated 1812, but none has been traced.

		V.G.	Fine	V.F.	E.F.	Unc.
52	Farthing 1813	$12.50	$17.50	$22.50	$30.00	$60.00
53	Halfpenny 1812	1.50	2.50	4.00	8.00	17.50
54	Halfpenny 1813	1.50	2.50	4.00	8.00	17.50

1814,
1 over 0

55	Penny 1812		Existence doubtful			
56	Penny 1813	3.00	5.00	8.00	12.50	25.00
57	Penny 1814	3.50	6.00	9.00	15.00	30.00
57a	Penny 1814, 2nd 1 over 0 . .	6.00	10.00	15.00	20.00	40.00

	V.G.	Fine	V.F.	E.F.	Unc.
58 Ship under topsails 1813...	$1.50	$2.50	$4.00	$8.00	$17.50

Broke Tokens of 1813

The Broke tokens were struck in honor of Captain P. B. Vere Broke, who commanded H.M.S. *Shannon* and captured U.S.S. *Chesapeake* in 1813. This was the first British naval victory in the War of 1812, and was thought worthy of commemoration by means of a coin.

Long bust   Short bust

59a   59

		V.G.	Fine	V.F.	E.F.	Unc.
59	Short bust, right ship higher	2.50	5.00	8.00	12.50	25.00
59a	Short bust, ships of equal height.................	4.50	7.50	11.00	15.00	35.00
59b	Long bust..............	4.00	7.00	10.00	14.00	30.00

Local Merchants' Tokens 1814-1820

In 1814 merchants began to issue tokens of their own design, a few being issued anonymously. There was a great variety of these pieces issued from 1814 to 1816, and in 1817 the government ordered their removal from circulation within three years because they had become too plentiful. Most were struck in England. The halfpenny inscribed, "For the Convenience of Trade" (61, 61a) was produced by William Mossop of Dublin. The Starr & Shannon tokens (75-77) may be the work of John Sheriff of Liverpool.

60   60a

		V.G.	Fine	V.F.	E.F.	Unc.
60	White's farthing, C of CHEAP above DR of DRY	$6.00	$8.00	$10.00	$20.00	$40.00
60a	White's, C above D	25.00	50.00	75.00		

61   62

61	For the Convenience of Trade 1814	7.00	9.00	12.50	20.00	40.00
61a	Same, brass	8.00	10.00	15.00	25.00	
62	Carritt & Alport 1814	3.50	6.00	9.00	12.50	25.00

The tokens 63 to 69 were engraved and struck by Thomas Halliday of Birmingham. Numbers 68-69 were issued by someone who objected to the appearance of brass and proclaimed his pieces to be "Genuine British Copper."

63   64

63	Hosterman & Etter 1814 . .	2.50	4.00	6.00	10.00	20.00
64	Hosterman & Etter 1815 . .	2.00	3.00	5.00	9.00	17.50

65	Halifax 1815	2.50	4.00	6.00	10.00	20.00

		V.G.	Fine	V.F.	E.F.	Unc.
66	Barry, large bust.........	$3.00	$5.00	$7.50	$12.50	$22.50
66a	Barry, slender bust.......	4.00	6.00	8.00	15.00	25.00
66b	Barry, short bust.........	2.50	4.00	6.00	10.00	20.00

67	Navigation & Trade 1815, small flag..............	2.50	4.00	6.00	10.00	20.00
67a	Same, large flag..........	3.00	5.00	7.50	12.50	22.50

68	British Copper 1815, large bust..............	2.00	3.50	5.00	10.00	20.00
68a	Same, slender bust........	2.00	3.50	5.00	10.00	20.00
68b	Same, small bust.........	3.00	5.00	7.50	12.50	25.00

69	British Copper on obv., 1815.................	7.50	10.00	15.00	22.50	35.00

The halfpenny of J. Brown (73) was once attributed to Scotland because of its design. The crude pieces 71 and 72 were made, probably locally, for J. Brown, and the bust and harp piece (70) may also have been made for him.

71   72

		V.G.	Fine	V.F.	E.F.	Unc.
70	Bust, harp in wreath......		Excessively rare			
71	Warehouse, harp in wreath.	—	—			
72	Script JB...............	—	—			

73

		V.G.	Fine	V.F.	E.F.	Unc.
73	J. Brown...............	$2.00	$3.50	$5.00	$10.00	$20.00

		V.G.	Fine	V.F.	E.F.	Unc.
74	Success, copper..........	9.00	12.50	17.50	25.00	50.00
74a	Success, brass............	12.50	17.50	22.50	30.00	60.00

75   76

		V.G.	Fine	V.F.	E.F.	Unc.
75	Commercial Change 1815..	2.50	4.00	6.00	11.50	20.00
76	Starr & Shannon 1815, thick flan..............	2.00	3.50	5.00	10.00	20.00
76a	Same, thin flan..........	2.00	3.50	5.00	10.00	20.00

	V.G.	Fine	V.F.	E.F.	Unc.
77 Starr & Shannon dies, no legends.............		Unique			

| **78** Miles W. White 1815...... | $2.50 | $4.00 | $6.00 | $11.50 | $20.00 |

| **79** Hardware 1816.......... | 2.50 | 4.00 | 6.00 | 11.50 | 20.00 |
| **80** W. A. & S. Black 1816.... | 3.00 | 5.00 | 7.50 | 12.50 | 25.00 |

The Trade & Navigation tokens of 1820 are attributed to Nova Scotia on account of this inscription. Since they are dated 1820, they would have been issued in violation of the law, for by 1820 all private tokens were to be out of circulation as required by a law passed in 1817. A variety with two shamrocks growing under the harp has been reported, but none has been seen in Canada.

| **81** Trade & Nav. 1820, copper | 3.00 | 5.00 | 7.50 | 12.50 | 25.00 |
| **81a** Same, brass............. | 5.00 | 7.50 | 10.00 | 15.00 | 30.00 |

Miscellaneous Tokens

The Robert Purves piece is an advertising card struck about 1857. Nova Scotia at this time had plenty of copper, so it is doubtful if this was ever intended to pass for a halfpenny. Besides it is too light in weight by Nova Scotia standards. Purves was a general merchant with shops in the towns of Wallace and Tatamagouche.

The Halifax ferry token may never have been used. It is believed to have been struck about 1845, for a roll was discovered in a wrapper dated 1846, when a safe deposit box in a trust company in Halifax was opened in 1941. Most specimens known today are in dull to bright red uncirculated condition.

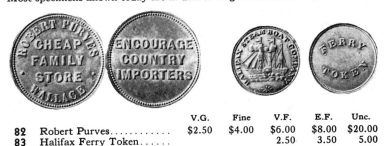

	V.G.	Fine	V.F.	E.F.	Unc.
82 Robert Purves	$2.50	$4.00	$6.00	$8.00	$20.00
83 Halifax Ferry Token			2.50	3.50	5.00

Semi-Regal Coins 1823-1856

The withdrawal of private tokens after 1817 created a fresh shortage of small change. Since it was impossible to obtain English regal copper, the government was permitted to issue copper coins of somewhat lighter weight and distinctive design to ensure local circulation. It was also planned to issue silver, but this idea was abandoned when it was learned that other British colonies had been refused permission to coin silver.

Thistle Tokens 1823-43

The first government or semi-regal coins were issued in 1823. These and the later issues through 1843 are known as the Thistle Tokens because of their reverse design. All issues were struck by John Walker & Co. of Birmingham. There was an issue of 400,000 halfpennies in 1823. The 1823 halfpenny of the finest workmanship is scarce. It is in higher relief, and the point of the bust is below the P in PROVINCE. In 1824 there was an issue of 217,776 pennies and 118,636 halfpennies.

In 1832 there was an issue of 200,000 pennies and 800,000 halfpennies. They bear the bust of George IV although coined two years after his death, because the order for coins similar in design to those of 1824 was taken too literally.

84   84a

		V.G.	Fine	V.F.	E.F.	Unc.
84	Halfpenny 1823.........	$2.00	$3.00	$5.00	$8.00	$30.00
84a	Same, finest workmanship.	3.00	4.00	6.00	12.00	35.00
84b	Same, no hyphen in Nova Scotia..........	4.00	5.00	7.00	15.00	40.00

85	Halfpenny 1824, P away from bust.............	4.00	6.50	9.00	17.50	50.00
85a	Same, with P close to bust.	4.00	6.50	9.00	17.50	60.00

86   86a   86b

86	Halfpenny 1832, left ribbon longer................	2.50	4.00	6.00	10.00	30.00
86a	Same, right ribbon longer..	2.00	3.00	5.00	8.50	25.00
86b	Same, ribbons equal length.	2.00	3.00	5.00	8.50	25.00

About 1835 struck counterfeits began to appear. They were made in Montreal and brought to Saint John, New Brunswick; from there they were passed to the fishermen in the Nova Scotia outports. They are lighter in weight and in bronze or brass. Nevertheless they were accepted in trade because of the continuing shortage of change.

The 1382 Counterfeit

The rare counterfeit dated 1382 is very much in demand. When the forgers saw that the date was transposed, they corrected it and continued to use the die. On this variety the date appears at a quick glance to be 1882. Fakes have been made of the 1382 coin by cutting open the 8 in the date of an original and sinking an 8 over the other 3. The fraud was easily discovered, for specimens bore a round-topped 3 in the date, were of pure copper and too heavy in weight. Both the originals and the struck counterfeits bear a flat-topped 3 in the date.

87a   87b   87c

		V.G.	Fine	V.F.	E.F.	Unc.
87	Counterfeit 1832.......... $	2.50 $	4.00 $	6.00 $	10.00	
87a	Counterfeit, flaw under nose	8.00	12.50	17.50	30.00	
87b	Counterfeit, dated 1382....	75.00	90.00	110.00	130.00	
87c	Counterfeit, corrected date.	8.00	12.50	17.50	30.00	

88	Penny 1824..............	4.00	6.00	9.00	15.00	30.00
89	Penny 1832..............	3.00	5.00	8.00	12.00	30.00
90	Counterfeit penny 1832....	3.00	5.00	8.00	12.00	

In 1840 and again in 1843 there were issues of 150,000 pennies and 300,000 halfpennies. The workmanship of these coins is variable, and the halfpennies of 1840 appear on flans of varying size and thickness. The weight, however, is not variable to the extent found in the case of private tokens. These pieces do not have a very flattering head of Queen Victoria. It is obviously an attempt to copy the young head designed by William Wyon for the English coinage.

91	Halfpenny 1840, large 0 ...	3.00	4.50	7.50	12.50	40.00
91a	Same, medium 0..........	2.00	3.00	5.00	8.00	25.00
91b	Same, small 0............	2.50	3.50	6.00	10.00	30.00
92	Halfpenny 1843	2.00	3.00	5.00	8.00	25.00

93   94

		V.G.	Fine	V.F.	E.F.	Unc.
93	Penny 1840..............	$2.50	$4.00	$ 6.00	$10.00	$30.00
94	Penny 1843, 3 over 0......	6.00	8.00	12.50	20.00	50.00
94a	Penny 1843, norm. date...	3.00	5.00	8.00	12.00	30.00

Mayflower Coinage 1856

This is one of the most beautiful of Canadian colonial coinages. The coins were engraved by L. C. Wyon and struck by Ralph Heaton & Sons of Birmingham. The obverse is Wyon's own design; the reverse was designed by John S. Thompson, a botanist of Halifax. The halfpennies with L.C.W. under the bust exist only in proof; some are mistaken for ordinary strikings, however, since early Heaton proofs were of inferior quality to those of the Royal Mint. The coinage comprised 150,000 pennies and 300,000 halfpennies.

95	Halfpenny 1856.........	2.25	4.00	6.00	9.00	30.00
95a	Same, LCW under bust (proofs only)..........				150.00	200.00
96	Penny 1856..............	3.00	5.00	8.00	12.00	30.00
96a	Same, LCW under bust...	3.00	5.00	8.00	12.00	30.00

Decimal Coinage 1861-1864

In 1859 Nova Scotia adopted a monetary system consisting of dollars and cents, but set its dollar at the rate of $5 per £ sterling. This enabled the province to utilize English silver (the shilling was equal to 25 cents and the 6d to $12\frac{1}{2}\cent$); however, it necessitated the issue of a half cent piece to make change for the 6d. Only cents and half cents were issued prior to Confederation in 1867.

½ CENT

The obverse, bearing a laureated bust of Victoria, is identical to that used for the New Brunswick coins of the same denomination and is one of those (Peck's obv. 3) for the English bronze farthing. The designer and engraver was L. C. Wyon.

The original pattern for the issue had a reverse device consisting of the Imperial crown and a wreath of roses and rose leaves; however, as an outgrowth of a propaganda campaign led by J. S. Thompson (father of Sir John Thompson), the wreath on the adopted issue consisted of both roses and mayflowers. The mayflower, *Epigea repens,* is the provincial flower.

Diameter: 20.65 mm; weight: 2.835 grams; composition: .950 copper, .040 tin, .010 zinc; edge: plain.

V.G. — Little detail to hair over ear or braid.
Fine — Strands of hair over ear begin to merge; braid is worn.
V.F. — Hair over ear is worn; braid is clear but no longer sharp.
E.F. — Slight wear on hair over ear; braid that holds knot in place is sharp and clear.

Date	Quan. Minted	Good	V.G.	Fine	V.F.	E.F.	Toned Unc.	Brill. Unc.
1861	400,000	$3.00	$4.00	$5.00	$6.00	$8.00	$15.00	$50.00
1864	400,000	3.00	4.00	5.00	6.00	8.00	15.00	50.00

1 CENT

The obverse is identical to that used for the New Brunswick coins of the same denomination and is one of those (Peck's obv. 6) used for the English bronze halfpence. The designer and engraver was L. C. Wyon. The wreath on the reverse contains both roses and mayflowers (see above), but differs slightly in arrangement from that on the half cent and the New Brunswick issue of the same denomination. The design was adapted from a model by C. Hill.

Specimens of the 1862 issue are quite scarce, suggesting that the reported mintage figure is incorrect. Perhaps the true figure is 100,000.

Diameter: 25.53 mm; weight: 5.670 grams; composition: .950 copper, .040 tin, .010 zinc; edge: plain.

1861	800,000	.50	1.00	1.75	3.75	6.50	14.00	50.00
1862	1,000,000	8.00	12.50	17.50	25.00	40.00	80.00	250.00
1864	800,000	.50	1.00	1.75	3.75	6.50	15.00	50.00

8

NEW BRUNSWICK

New Brunswick was claimed by France as part of Acadia. It was not settled until 1631, when a fort was built at the mouth of the St. John River. When Acadia was ceded to Great Britain in 1713, the French continued to dispute the British claim to New Brunswick, but gave up all claims in 1763.

Under British rule it was governed from Nova Scotia until 1784, when it was detached from Nova Scotia at the request of the inhabitants. New Brunswick was not as seriously short of coin as were the other colonies. A brisk trade with Nova Scotia kept the colony supplied to a limited extent with copper. The need for copper was not serious before 1830, when a halfpenny was anonymously issued at Saint John.

Miscellaneous Tokens ca. 1830-1845

The first piece was not issued because the name of the city was spelled incorrectly. Saint John is the largest city of New Brunswick, and in those days was the capital. St. John's is the capital of Newfoundland. Evidently this rarity was made by the manufacturers of the almost equally rare Montreal Ropery halfpenny.

The second piece appeared about 1830. Its obverse die was used also for an anonymous token issued at the same time in Lower Canada (140a).

The McDermott token is an advertising card, struck in brass. It was always thought to have been issued about 1855, but recent research suggests that it may have appeared ten years or so earlier. It is too small to have been used as a halfpenny.

	V.G.	Fine	V.F.	E.F.	Unc.
97 St. John's N.B.		Very rare			

		V.G.	Fine	V.F.	E.F.	Unc.
98	For Public Accommodation	$7.50	$11.50	$15.00	$20.00	$40.00
99	McDermott business card..	50.00	75.00	100.00	125.00	200.00

Semi-Regal Coins 1843-1854

New Brunswick issued its first semi-regal copper in 1843. The coins were struck by Boulton & Watt of Soho, and depict a diademed head of Queen Victoria, to which the Colonial Office objected. The coins, however, were allowed to circulate. It is at present not known how many coins were struck, but their availability today suggests that the issue was the same size as that of 1854.

		V.G.	Fine	V.F.	E.F.	Unc.
100	Halfpenny 1843.	$1.50	$2.50	$4.00	$8.00	$30.00

101	Penny 1843.	2.00	3.50	5.00	10.00	30.00

In 1853 the New Brunswick Governor applied to the English government for a fresh coinage of pence and halfpence. The 1843 matrices (and punches?) were forwarded to the Royal Mint, where they were used as a source of modified designs. These alterations, probably by L. C. Wyon, consisted of the substitution on the obverse of William Wyon's portrait for the English shilling on the halfpenny and that for the English halfpenny on the penny. In addition, the word CURRENCY was used in place of TOKEN on the reverse. The use of CURRENCY indicated the official nature of the issue and also implied Halifax Currency, the standard at the time. Due to a heavy schedule at the Royal Mint, the new dies were sent to the Heaton Mint, where 480,000 pieces of each denomination were struck.

		V.G.	Fine	V.F.	E.F.	Unc.
102	Halfpenny 1854..........	$1.50	$3.00	$5.00	$10.00	$35.00

103	Penny 1854, heavy flag....	2.50	4.00	6.00	12.50	35.00
103a	Penny 1854, light flag.....	2.50	4.00	6.00	12.50	35.00

Decimal Coinage 1861-1864

½ CENT

In 1860 New Brunswick adopted a monetary system consisting of dollars and cents, setting the dollar equal to the United States gold dollar. This made the English shilling worth slightly more than 24 cents and the 6d slightly more than 12 cents. Consequently, a half cent piece was not required to make change for the latter denomination.

Although New Brunswick did not need and in fact did not order an issue of this denomination, the Royal Mint struck over 200,000 pieces for the province. The mistake was soon discovered and most of the coins went to the melting pot. The only ones to escape were a few proofs and an unknown number (perhaps a few hundred) that were mixed with the Nova Scotia half cents and sent to Halifax.

The obverse design is identical to that used for the Nova Scotia coins of the same denomination and is one of those (Peck's obv. 3) for the English bronze farthing.

The reverse is similar to that for the Nova Scotia half cent.

Diameter: 20.65 mm; weight: 2.835 grams; composition: .950 copper, .040 tin, .010 zinc; edge: plain.

G. — *Hair over ear worn through.*
V.G. — *Little detail to hair over ear or braid.*
Fine — *Strands of hair over ear begin to merge; braid is worn.*
V.F. — *Hair over ear is worn; braid is clear but no longer sharp.*
E.F. — *Slight wear on hair over ear; braid that holds knot in place is sharp and clear.*

Date	Quan. Minted	Good	V.G.	Fine	V.F.	E.F.	Unc.	Brill. Unc.
1861	222,800	$15.00	$25.00	$30.00	$40.00	$55.00	$95.00	$250.00

1 CENT

The obverse is identical to that for the Nova Scotia coins of the same denomination and is one of those (Peck's obv. 6) used for the English halfpenny. The designer and engraver was L. C. Wyon.

The reverse design is very similar to that used for the Nova Scotia issue; the wreath differs only in minor respects. The design was adapted from a model by C. Hill.

Diameter: 25.53 mm; weight: 5.670 grams; composition: .950 copper, .040 tin, .010 zinc; edge: plain.

Short tip 6   Long tip 6

Date	Approx. Minted	Good	V.G.	Fine	V.F.	E.F.	Unc.	Brill. Unc.
1861	1,000,000	.40	.85	1.25	2.00	3.25	12.50	30.00
1864								
short tip 6	1,000,000	.40	.85	1.25	2.00	3.25	12.50	30.00
long tip 6		.40	.85	1.25	2.00	3.25	12.50	30.00

5 CENTS

The obverse, designed and engraved by L. C. Wyon, has a portrait of Victoria that would later be used on the Dominion of Canada issues (Portrait 2).

The reverse wreath is of maple; the design is identical to that used for the Province of Canada five cents of 1858.

Diameter: 15.49 mm; weight: 1.162 grams; composition: .925 silver, .075 copper; edge: reeded.

G. — *Hair over ear worn through.*
V.G. — *No details in hair over ear; jewels in diadem partly worn away.*
Fine — *Strands of hair over ear begin to merge; jewels slightly blurred.*
V.F. — *Hair and the jewels clear but not sharp.*
E.F. — *Braid is slightly worn but generally sharp and clear.*

Small 6

Large 6

Date	Approx. Minted	Good	V.G.	Fine	V.F.	E.F.	Unc.
1862 100,000		$5.00	$10.00	$15.00	$30.00	$45.00	$100.00
1864 small 6 .... ⎫ 100,000		4.00	9.00	15.00	30.00	45.00	100.00
large 6 .... ⎭		7.50	15.00	20.00	40.00	60.00	125.00

10 CENTS

The obverse is virtually identical to and was derived from Canadian Portrait 6 (that particular Canadian obverse existed long before it appeared on the issues of 1892). The designer and engraver was L. C. Wyon.

The reverse design, the device of which is a wreath of maple surmounted by the St. Edward's crown, is identical to that used for the Province of Canada ten cents of 1858.

Diameter: 17.91 mm; weight: 2.324 grams; composition: .925 silver, .075 copper; edge: reeded.

                        Normal 2   Double-punched 2

1862 norm. date . ⎫ 150,000		4.00	7.50	15.00	30.00	50.00	110.00
dbl.-pun. 2 . ⎭		4.00	7.50	15.00	30.00	50.00	110.00
1864 150,000		3.00	6.00	12.50	25.00	40.00	100.00

20 CENTS

The obverse, designed and engraved by L. C. Wyon, has a portrait that is similar to that on the Province of Canada issue of the same denomination.

The reverse is also similar to that used for the Province of Canada issue and, indeed, was probably initially intended for that coin. The designer and engraver may have been L. C. Wyon, but this is not known with certainty.

Diameter: 22.99 mm; weight: 4.648 grams; composition: .925 silver, .075 copper; edge: reeded.

1862 150,000		3.50	6.00	9.00	12.50	20.00	100.00
1864 150,000		3.50	6.00	9.00	12.50	20.00	100.00

9

LOWER CANADA

New France was conquered by the British in 1760 and ceded to Great Britain in 1763. It was known as the colony of Quebec until 1791. Originally the colony included the St. Lawrence basin and the Great Lakes region, and large areas of territory extending south to the Ohio River. In 1783 the Great Lakes and the upper St. Lawrence were made the boundary with the United States. In 1791 the Great Lakes area was separated from Quebec, which now became the colony of Lower Canada. Lower Canada was predominantly French, and was the largest and most populous of the Canadian colonies.

Wellington Tokens

No special coinage was struck for Lower Canada until 1837. About 1813 anonymous tokens began to appear. The earliest were the Wellington tokens, brought over by British troops sent to Canada to fight the Americans in 1814. These tokens depicted a bust of the Duke of Wellington, and were very popular. They were often struck over other tokens. Some of them are antedated in order to evade laws passed in 1825 against private tokens.

The "Battle" tokens (111-113) were struck by Sir Edward Thomason of Birmingham for J. K. Picard of Hull in honor of Wellington's many victories in Portugal and Spain. Specimens in silver were struck for presentation at Court, Picard having been invited by the Prince Regent to come to London and show his coppers. Note that only on 112b is the Spanish word *Ciudad* (City) spelled correctly. Brass counterfeits appeared in Canada after the originals were brought out.

		V.G.	Fine	V.F.	E.F.	Unc.
109	Wellington Hibernia 1805..	$4.00	$6.00	$8.00	$13.50	$30.00
110	Trade & Commerce 1811 ..	12.00	15.00	20.00	30.00	60.00
111	Cuidad-Salamanca, copper.	1.50	2.50	4.00	7.00	12.50
111a	Same, silver..............	50.00	65.00	80.00	100.00	175.00
111b	Counterfeit, brass........	3.00	5.00	8.00		

		Obverse	112	113

		V.G.	Fine	V.F.	E.F.	Unc.
112	Cuidad-Madrid, copper....	$ 1.50	$ 2.50	$ 4.00	$ 7.00	$12.50
112a	Same, silver..............	65.00	80.00	100.00	150.00	200.00
112b	Ciudad (correct spelling), copper................	8.00	10.00	15.00	22.50	40.00
113	Salamanca-Pampluno.....	1.50	2.50	5.00	7.50	17.50

Numbers 114-121 were all designed by Thomas Halliday, the Cossack penny being considered an example of his best work. Of these pieces, most varieties of 114-117 were struck over Guppy tokens of Bristol. It is interesting to note that specimens of 117a were overstruck with other designs for use in England, proving that not all the anonymous Wellington tokens of these listed types were sent to Canada.

The pennies 118-120 are called the Peninsular Pennies because they were struck by Sir Edward Thomason for use by Wellington's troops in Portugal and Spain. They were designed so that they could not be mistaken for English, Spanish, or Portuguese copper. The reverse of 120 is a tribute to the Russian Cossacks, who gave Napoleon's Grande Armée such an uncomfortable time in Russia in 1812 and 1813.

114
←

115
→

114	Britannia 1813, thick flan..	1.50	2.00	4.00	7.50	17.50
114a	Britannia 1813, thin flan...	1.50	2.00	4.00	7.50	17.50
115	Undated, with trident.....	1.50	2.00	4.00	7.50	17.50

115a
←

115b
→

115a	Britannia with spear......	2.50	3.00	5.00	10.00	25.00
115b	Bold lettering............	1.50	2.00	4.00	7.50	17.50

116

	V.G.	Fine	V.F.	E.F.	Unc.
116 Field Marshal, rev. wreath.	$35.00	$50.00	$75.00	$100.00	—

Obverse   117   117a

117 Penny, fine lettering	12.00	15.00	20.00	30.00	50.00
117a Penny, bold lettering	12.00	15.00	20.00	30.00	50.00

118 Penny 1813, date under bust	12.00	15.00	18.00	25.00	45.00

Number 121 (Breton 968) is of doubtful existence. It would be, if it does exist, a mule of a Wellington obverse with a reverse depicting the seated figure of Commerce as seen on the Tiffin pennies (156-159). It has been suggested that the penny with the legends in fine lettering (117) may have been intended by Breton to be 968, as a drawing of this variety is missing from Breton's work.

119   120

		V.G.	Fine	V.F.	E.F.	Unc.
119	Penny 1813, date on rev...	$8.00	$10.00	$14.00	$18.00	$30.00
120	Cossack penny..........	10.00	12.50	15.00	20.00	45.00
121	Penny 1812..............		Existence doubted			

The Marquis Wellington halfpenny was struck by Isaac Parkes of Dublin. It is antedated, since Wellington did not become a marquis until 1814. The tokens of 1814, struck on Canadian order, also were antedated to evade the law against private tokens.

| 122 | Marquis Wellington 1813.. | 3.00 | 5.00 | 7.50 | 10.00 | 25.00 |

123   124a

123	½ Penny Token, rev. wreath...............	7.00	10.00	15.00	25.00	—
124	Round epaulette 1814.....	1.50	2.50	4.00	7.50	15.00
124a	Square epaulette 1814.....	1.50	2.50	4.00	7.50	15.00

The halfpenny tokens dated 1815 and 1816 are lightweight pieces struck on Canadian order and issued about 1830. Those of 1816 were designed by Halliday.

		V.G.	Fine	V.F.	E.F.	Unc.
125	Wellington Waterloo 1815, Bust.............	$3.00	$5.00	$7.50	$11.50	$25.00
126	Wellington Waterloo 1815, Ship..............	2.00	3.50	5.00	8.00	20.00

127	Waterloo 1816, 10 strings..	2.00	3.50	5.00	8.00	20.00
127a	Same, 8 strings..........	2.25	4.00	6.00	9.00	22.50
128	Wellington Montreal 1816.	2.50	3.50	5.00	7.50	20.00

Anonymous Tokens

About the time of the introduction of the Wellington tokens, anonymous tokens began to appear in circulation. Some were English and Irish pieces imported after use in the British Isles, while others were struck on Canadian order. In 1825 the governments of Upper and Lower Canada passed laws forbidding the further import of private tokens. The law was carelessly worded, for it was soon discovered that its provisions did not extend to tokens undated or dated before 1825. The law was never amended to correct this fault, evidently, and after 1825 Lower Canada especially was flooded with anonymous metallic trash.

The Hibernia penny (129) is an anonymous Irish token designed by Peter Wyon. The Victoria Nobis Est halfpenny was struck over Guppy tokens.

129	Hibernia penny 1805......	12.50	16.00	22.50	30.00	50.00

		V.G.	Fine	V.F.	E.F.	Unc.
130	Victoria Nobis Est........	$2.00	$3.00	$5.00	$8.00	$20.00

The original Britannia-eagle tokens of 1813 were struck over Guppy tokens of Bristol, probably for a Boston merchant who settled in Montreal in 1813. These halfpennies were popular, and were later imitated (131a-133) on thinner flans. Most of the 1815 tokens were discovered about 1900, when a barrel of them in their pristine beauty was found during the demolition of an old building.

131	Eagle 1813, original.......	2.00	3.00	5.00	8.00	20.00
131a	Eagle 1813, counterfeit....	4.00	7.00	10.00	13.50	
132	Eagle 1814..............	2.00	3.00	4.50	7.50	
133	Eagle 1815..............	1.50	2.00	3.00	4.50	7.00

The halfpennies and farthings (135-139c) are all lightweight pieces imported into Canada about 1830. Numbers 135-139c have been found in hoards in the Province of Quebec, indicating that they were intended for use in Lower Canada. It has not been possible to identify the busts on these coins, although attempts to do so have been made. It has been suggested that 138 and 138a bear the bust of Col. de Salaberry, but this cannot be proved.

It is interesting to note that among the coins in a large hoard found in Quebec was a variety of the Ships Colonies & Commerce token. This piece, No. 135, has always been considered a variety of Breton 997, but it portrays a very different ship. The hull is much shorter than on the varieties of Breton 997, and the water is very rough. This ship is also seen on No. 126, the Wellington Waterloo 1815 token, which uses the bust of No. 136. It has been implied in the past that 138b is a fake.

135

	V.G.	Fine	V.F.	E.F.	Unc.
135 SHIPS COLONIES & COMMERCE, short hull..............	$2.50	$3.50	$5.00	$7.50	$20.00

136
←

136b
→

136 Bust with open sleeve.....	2.50	3.50	5.00	7.50	20.00
136a Bust with closed sleeve....	6.00	9.00	12.50	17.50	35.00
136b Small bust, broad rim.....	10.00	15.00	20.00	30.00	50.00

137 Commercial Change.......	2.00	3.50	6.00	9.00	20.00
137a Commercial Change, large bust..............	12.50	15.00	20.00	30.00	50.00

138 Trade 1825, open sleeve...	1.50	2.50	4.00	6.00	15.00
138a Trade 1825, closed sleeve..	2.00	3.00	5.00	7.50	20.00
138b Trade 1825, bust of 136...		Extremely rare			

139 Bust 1820, thick flan......	1.50	2.00	4.00	6.00	15.00
139a Same, thin flan...........	1.50	2.00	4.00	6.00	15.00
139b Bust 1820, lg. date, copper.	3.00	5.00	8.00	12.50	
139c Same, brass..............	2.00	4.00	7.00	10.00	

The halfpennies inscribed "For Public Accommodation" were issued about 1830, and were struck by the manufacturers of the token of Saint John, New Brunswick. The variety with large periods has heavy limbs on the letters E in the inscription of the obverse. The variety with small periods has E's with light limbs.

		V.G.	Fine	V.F.	E.F.	Unc.
140	Public Accommodation, large periods	$2.00	$3.00	$4.00	$6.00	$18.00
140a	Same, small periods	2.00	3.00	4.00	6.00	18.00

Private Tokens

The private tokens bearing their issuers' names are extremely variable in weight and quality. The only really honest token in this regard is the Molson halfpenny of 1837. The Montreal Ropery halfpenny was issued about 1824, shortly before the firm changed hands. The Mullins token was issued in anticipation that the son would enter into partnership, but this did not happen.

| **141** | Montreal Ropery . . . . | 300.00 | 450.00 | 600.00 | 750.00 | |
| **142** | Mullins & Son . . . . | 4.00 | 6.00 | 8.00 | 10.00 | 25.00 |

The "Canada" tokens of 1830 and 1841, although seemingly anonymous, are known to have been issued by James Duncan, a hardware merchant of Montreal. He later settled in Charlottetown, Prince Edward Island, where he circulated these pieces until issuing his "cents" in 1855 (Nos. 48-51).

| **143** | Canada 1830 . . . . | 2.00 | 3.50 | 5.00 | 7.00 | 20.00 |
| **144** | Canada 1841 . . . . | 2.00 | 3.50 | 5.00 | 7.00 | 20.00 |

T. S. Brown, the issuer of 145, was a hardware merchant who took up arms in the Rebellion of 1837, and had to flee to the United States when the rebellion was put down. He remained there until amnesty was granted in 1844.

John Shaw's halfpenny was issued at Quebec in 1837. Shaw withdrew his tokens when the Quebec Bank issued its Habitant coins the following year.

145a

		V.G.	Fine	V.F.	E.F.	Unc.
145	Brown, S away from o of Co.	$1.50	$2.50	$4.00	$6.00	$20.00
145a	Brown, S close to o	1.50	2.50	4.00	6.00	20.00

The Molson halfpenny was struck in Montreal by Jean Marie Arnault, who also engraved the dies, probably from designs submitted by the Company. The obverse is a copy in reverse of that of a halfpenny token issued in Perth, Scotland, in 1797.

146	Shaw, Quebec............	2.00	3.00	4.50	7.00	25.00
147	Molson, thick flan........	25.00	30.00	40.00	50.00	100.00
147a	Molson, thin flan........	30.00	40.00	50.00	60.00	125.00

The Roy token was issued in 1837. Specimens on thin flans were made by a journeyman employed by the manufacturer. This individual would run off a few extra specimens from the dies whenever he needed money for liquor. The appearance of these lightweight sous forced Roy to withdraw his tokens to avoid discredit.

148	J. Roy, thick flan........	7.00	10.00	15.00	20.00
148a	J. Roy, thin flan.........	7.00	10.00	15.00	20.00

The Bust and Harp Tokens 1820-1825

These halfpennies first appeared in Lower Canada in 1825. The originals were struck in Dublin in 1825, the first specimens bearing that date. On learning of the laws passed in Canada against the further import of anonymous tokens, the manufacturers altered the date on the die to 1820 and completed the order, and the coins were smuggled into Canada.

They were very popular, especially among the Irish immigrants to Lower Canada, and in a few years thousands of brass imitations appeared and became a nuisance. The original issue in copper was rather small, the 1825 halfpenny being very rare. The overdate 1820 over 1825 is even more so. Fakes have been made of the 1825 halfpenny by altering the date on brass imitations, but these were soon exposed because of their inferior workmanship and their being made of brass.

Copper Originals

		V.G.	Fine	V.F.	E.F.	Unc.
149	Bust and harp 1825.......	$75.00	$90.00	$125.00	$175.00	
150	Same, 1820, 0 over 5......	—	—	—	—	
150a	Same, 1820, norm. date...	2.50	4.00	7.50	12.50	

151a   152a

Varieties of Brass Imitations

		V.G.	Fine	V.F.	E.F.	Unc.
151	Small bust, 10 strings.....	1.00	2.00	3.50	5.00	12.00
151a	Same, 9 strings...........	1.00	2.00	3.50	5.00	12.00
151b	Same, 8 strings...........	2.00	3.00	5.00	7.00	20.00
152	Large bust, 10 strings.....	1.00	2.00	3.50	5.00	12.00
152a	Same, 9 strings...........	2.00	3.00	5.00	7.00	20.00

153   154

		V.G.	Fine	V.F.	E.F.	Unc.
153	Crude, 8 strings..........	$2.50	$4.00	$6.00	$8.00	
153a	Same, copper.............	3.00	5.00	7.50	10.00	
154	Bust & harp to right, copper	—	—	—		

The Tiffin Tokens

About 1832 a Montreal grocer named Joseph Tiffin imported a series of anonymous English tokens. These came to be called "Tiffins" by collectors in Canada. They were designed by Thomas Halliday and struck in Birmingham. A few penny tokens of similar design, also by Halliday, appeared at the same time in Canada. These pieces were at once readily accepted because of their good weight, but it was not long before imitations began to appear in change. At first these copies were in lightweight copper, of reasonably good fabric, but soon the country was cursed with a flood of brass imitations of extremely variable workmanship.

Copper Originals

155	Halfpenny 1812..........	1.50	2.00	3.50	5.00	15.00

157, 158 obv.   156, 157 rev.

156	Penny, 1812 on reverse....	2.50	4.00	6.00	9.00	20.00
157	Penny, 1812 on both sides.	2.50	4.00	6.00	9.00	20.00
158	Penny, 1812 on obverse...	2.50	4.00	6.00	9.00	20.00
159	Penny, 1813 on obverse...	3.50	5.00	9.00	15.00	30.00

Imitation Halfpennies

160	Halfpenny 1812, copper...	1.50	2.00	3.50	5.00	15.00

	161	161a	161b

		V.G.	Fine	V.F.	E.F.	Unc.
161	Medium bust 1812, brass ..	$1.25	$1.75	$2.75	$5.00	
161a	Large bust 1812, brass	1.50	2.00	3.50	5.00	
161b	Small bust 1812, brass.....	1.25	1.75	2.75	5.00	

162	Medium bust, no value 1812, brass.................	1.25	1.75	2.75	5.00
162a	Large bust, no value 1812, brass.................	1.50	2.00	3.50	5.00

The rare "Bon Pour Deux Sous" penny is probably a pattern for a Canadian token. The last two pennies are anonymous pieces with obverses related to those of this series.

163

163	BON POUR DEUX SOUS penny 1812............		Very rare			
164	Commerce...............	6.00	10.00	15.00	20.00	45.00
165	Commerce 1814	5.00	8.00	12.50	17.50	30.00

The "Blacksmith" Tokens

Some time after 1830, an enterprising blacksmith of Montreal developed a
new counterfeiting technique. He drank to excess, and therefore made his
own halfpennies to buy his liquor. His forgeries were clever imitations of
the battered, worn-out, old English and Irish regal halfpennies of George III,
which were the only legal copper currency at the time.

The technique was to leave the dies unfinished. An outline of a bust was
cut on one side, and an incomplete Britannia or harp on the other, with no
inscriptions nor date. To further heighten the appearance of age and wear,
the coins were overheated to darken them before being passed into circulation. Soon the technique was taken up by others, and these "Blacksmith"
tokens, as collectors call them, flooded the country.

The series was almost completely ignored by the earlier writers, Breton
including only two in his work. They were described in detail by Howland
Wood, whose 1910 monograph is still the standard reference.

166   166a

	Wood Nos.		Fair	Good	V.G.
166	1-4	Bust left, rev. Britannia, copper	$2.00	$3.00	$4.00
166a	11	Same, incomplete bust	2.00	3.00	4.00
166b	13-18	Similar, brass	1.50	2.50	3.50

167a   168

167	5, 6	Bust left, rev. harp, copper	3.00	5.00	8.00
167a	12	Same, incomplete bust	2.00	3.00	4.00
168	7	"Britannia on water," copper	4.00	7.00	10.00
168a	8	Same, brass	4.00	7.00	10.00

Among the pieces of atrocious style which now began to curse the colony
were imitations of the Tiffin tokens (169-169b), the Bust & Harp tokens (170),
the Ships Colonies & Commerce tokens (171-173), and other imitations of
English coins (257-259).

169

170

Wood Nos.			Fair	Good	V.G.
169	19	Long chin, copper..................	$50.00	$75.00	$100.00
169a	20	Long chin, brass...................	50.00	75.00	100.00
169b	21	Weak chin.......................	65.00	90.00	125.00
170	22	Weak chin, rev. harp..............	75.00	125.00	175.00

171

172

171	9	Bust and ship.....................	100.00	125.00	200.00
172	—	Ship with drooping flag............	5.00	8.00	12.00

173

174

173	10	Harp obverse......................	30.00	45.00	60.00
174	23	Bust right, rev. Britannia...........	1.50	2.50	4.00

175

176

Wood Nos.			Fair	Good	V.G.
175	33	GLORIOUS III VIS — BITIT............	$ 1.50	$ 2.50	$ 4.00
176	34	Similar, types facing opposite.......	75.00	125.00	200.00
177	35	Similar, rev. harp.................	75.00	125.00	200.00

178	32	Union Jack shield, rev. anchor.......	50.00	75.00	100.00

The Vexator Canadiensis Tokens

These are among the strangest pieces to have been issued anywhere in the world. They appeared some time after 1830, and are satirical pieces exceedingly cleverly designed to evade the laws against forgery, sedition, and the issue of private tokens.

To ensure that they would be accepted in change, the coins bore a bust on the obverse and a seated female figure on the reverse, thus superficially resembling English regal copper. To avoid being prosecuted for forgery, the issuers made use of inscriptions quite different from those seen on regal copper.

They are satirical pieces in that the types are caricatures and the legends definitely provocative. The obverse legend as usually read means, "The Tormentor of Canada." The reverse legend means, "Wouldn't you like to catch them?" and could allude to those who put the coins into circulation. However, the toils of the law were foreseen here and cleverly avoided. The third letter in the obverse legend is very vague in form, and could easily be an N as an X. The word could then be read as VENATOR and the legend translated as "A Canadian Trapper." The bust is very shaggy and appears to be wearing a fur cap such as trappers wore in those days. The reverse legend could as easily have referred to fur-bearing animals as to the issuers of the coins. Thus, if caught, the issuers could plead that the coins were really medalets honoring the fur trade, of which Montreal was in those days an important center.

The date 1811 is clearly an antedate. After going to all the trouble to evade prosecution for forgery and sedition, the issuers were not going to run afoul of the law of 1825 against private tokens. This method of evasion was very easy. The light and variable weight of these coins also indicates that they are antedated, for nothing as light as these would have been acceptable in 1811.

Who was the "Tormentor of Canada?" Since the coins are antedated, it certainly was not Sir James Craig, autocratic though he was. It probably was King William IV, whose attitude toward colonies, especially those acquired from other countries in warfare, was very harsh. Almost any of the governors of Lower Canada from 1830 to 1838, or some particularly obnoxious local officials of the period, also could have qualified for this dubious title.

The fur-trade aspect of these coins is the fruit of brilliant reasoning by Dr. J. P. C. Kent of the British Museum and R. H. M. Dolley of Belfast. The evasion of the laws against forgery was suggested to the author by R. C.

Bell of Newcastle-on-Tyne, who pointed out that it was in the technique of the makers of the old English "Bungtown" tokens. It had been known since the time of R. W. McLachlan that these coins were antedated, but the fact had been almost forgotten in recent years.

		Fair	Good	V.G.
179	CANADIN SIS, copper....................	$15.00	$25.00	$35.00
179a	Same, brass............................	30.00	50.00	75.00
180	CANADIENSIS, copper....................	15.00	25.00	35.00
180a	Same, brass...........................	30.00	50.00	75.00

The First Bank Tokens 1835-1837
Bank of Montreal

In 1835 the banks refused to take any more anonymous brass pieces and other metallic trash except by weight. To supply a copper coinage, the Bank of Montreal began issuing halfpenny tokens of good weight. The value was inscribed in French on the reverse, but was incorrectly expressed by the plural form SOUS rather than SOU. This did not hinder their circulation at all. In 1836 the bank received government authority to supply copper, and added its name to the reverse inscriptions; but did not correct the value, for the error was taken by everyone as a guarantee of authenticity. The Bank of Montreal sous were struck in Birmingham. Each year there was an issue of about 72,000.

		V.G.	Fine	V.F.	E.F.	Unc.
181	Bank Token Montreal.....	$1.25	$2.50	$4.00	$6.00	$20.00
182	Bank of Montreal Token ..	1.25	2.50	4.00	6.00	20.00

Banque du Peuple

The first sou of the Banque du Peuple was the so-called "Rebellion sou," issued in 1837. It received its name because of the addition of a small star and a liberty cap on the reverse, said to have been done at the instigation of an accountant who favored the cause of the rebels of 1837. It was soon discovered, and the coin was replaced with another type in 1838. The Rebellion sou was engraved by Jean Marie Arnault of Montreal, who struck about 12,000 pieces. There is considerable variation in size and weight.

The second sou of the Banque du Peuple (184-184a) was issued in 1838 to replace the Rebellion sou. It was struck in Belleville, New Jersey, and about 84,000 were struck.

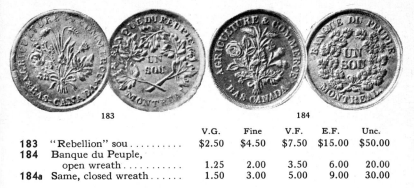

183   184

		V.G.	Fine	V.F.	E.F.	Unc.
183	"Rebellion" sou	$2.50	$4.50	$7.50	$15.00	$50.00
184	Banque du Peuple,					
	open wreath	1.25	2.00	3.50	6.00	20.00
184a	Same, closed wreath	1.50	3.00	5.00	9.00	30.00

City Bank

The two rare pieces 185 and 186 are supposed to be patterns for and issue of sous by the City Bank. Both were produced in Montreal by Jean Marie Arnault. Evidently the bank decided to abandon the issue of sous in favor of participation in the issue of the Habitant coppers.

185   186

185	Pro Bono Publico 1837		Unique		
186	Bank Token ½ Penny	250.00	300.00	350.00	500.00	—

Bouquet Sous

The Bouquet Sous are imitations of the Bank of Montreal tokens. The latter pieces were so popular that lightweight imitations soon appeared, bearing a similar obverse bouquet of roses, thistles, shamrocks, and wheat. Inscriptions were entirely in French, however (with the words AGRICULTURE and COMMERCE the same in both languages), and the value was correctly rendered in the singular.

Because of the wide usage of the Bouquet Sous, they became the first series to achieve great popularity with collectors. They have been more thoroughly studied than other colonial issues, and it has been traditional to collect them by die variety. Various authors have published detailed listings, and more than a dozen different numbering systems have been proposed over the years. P. N. Breton's 1894 listing remains the most popular and it was felt best to use his numbers here for simplicity.

Bouquet Sous are most easily identified by first counting the number of leaves in the reverse wreath. This number will serve to locate a general area in one of the three groups below, after which details may be compared with the notes below the illustrations. Such points as the number and location of shamrocks and relative position of letters, berries, and leaves will serve as guides to identification.

I. Belleville Issues

The Belleville mint was a private company in Belleville, New Jersey, whose production was mainly American tokens. Number 670 is a mule which combines a normal obverse with the reverse of a token intended for a Belleville merchant, T. D. Seaman. This reverse had been rejected because the name was incorrectly rendered as "T. Duseaman."

Obv. 1 —
3 shamrocks
at right

Rev. A —
"T. Duseaman
Butcher"

Breton No.		V.G.	Fine	V.F.	E.F.	Unc.
670	Obv. 1, rev. A.............	$3.00	$5.00	$8.00	$12.00	$35.00

Sixteen leaves in reverse wreath

Obv. 2 — 3 sham-
rocks right, 1 left

Obv. 3 — 2 sham-
rocks right, 1 left

Obv. 4 — 3 sham-
rocks right, 1 left

Obv. 5 — 4 sham-
rocks right, 3 left

Obv. 6 — 2 sham-
rocks left, none right

Rev. B — berries   Rev. C — no berry   Rev. D — no berry
each side of bow   left of bow   right of bow

Breton No.		V.G.	Fine	V.F.	E.F.	Unc.
675	Obv. 2, rev. B............	$100.00	$150.00	$200.00	$275.00	
676	Obv. 3, rev. B............	7.00	10.00	13.00	18.00	$40.00
677	Obv. 4, rev. B............	60.00	85.00	110.00	150.00	
678	Obv. 4, rev. C............	1.50	2.50	3.50	5.00	20.00
679	Obv. 5, rev. C............	1.50	2.50	3.50	5.00	20.00
680	Obv. 6, rev. C............	2.00	4.00	6.00	9.00	30.00
681	Obv. 1, rev. D............	35.00	50.00	75.00	100.00	150.00
682	Obv. 3, rev. D............	7.00	10.00	15.00	20.00	50.00

(Also see No. 674)

Seventeen leaves in reverse wreath

Obv. 6

Rev. E —
17 leaves,
no bow

683	Obv. 6, rev. E............	3.50	5.00	8.00	12.00	35.00

(Also see No. 684)

Eighteen leaves in reverse wreath, no bow

Rev. F — berry   Rev. G — berry   Obv. 7 — 3 sham-   Rev. H — no berry
left of bottom N   over bottom N   rocks right, 2 left   near bottom N

685	Obv. 1, rev. F............	6.00	9.00	12.00	15.00	45.00
686	Obv. 1, rev. G............	2.00	4.00	6.00	10.00	30.00
687	Obv. 5, rev. H............	2.00	4.00	6.00	10.00	30.00
688	Obv. 7, rev. H............	2.00	4.00	6.00	10.00	30.00

(Also see Nos. 689-690)

Eighteen leaves in reverse wreath, with bow

Obv. 8 — 3 sham-
rocks right, 2 left

Obv. 9 — 2 sham-
rocks left, none right

Obv. 10 — rose
at left

Obv. 11 — 1 sham-
rock right, 1 left

Obv. 12 — 2 sham-
rocks right, none left

Obv. 13 — 1 sham-
rock left, none right

Obv. 14 — "broken"
leaf above thistles

Rev. J — letters
EAL double-punched

Rev. K — no
center dot

Rev. L — with dot,
UN near SOU

Rev. M — with dot
UN far from SOU

Breton No.		V.G.	Fine	V.F.	E.F.	Unc.
692	Obv. 5, rev. J............	$2.00	$4.00	$6.00	$10.00	$30.00
693	Obv. 7, rev. J............	2.00	4.00	6.00	10.00	30.00
694	Obv. 8, rev. J............	2.00	4.00	6.00	10.00	30.00

Breton No.		V.G.	Fine	V.F.	E.F.	Unc.
695	Obv. 6, rev. J............	$ 2.00	$ 4.00	$ 6.00	$10.00	$30.00
696	Obv. 6, rev. K..........	8.00	11.00	15.00	20.00	40.00
697	Obv. 9, rev. L..........	4.00	6.00	8.00	12.00	35.00
698	Obv. 10, rev. L.........	6.00	9.00	13.00	20.00	40.00
699	Obv. 10, rev. M.........	3.00	5.00	8.00	12.00	35.00
700	Obv. 11, rev. M.........	2.00	4.00	6.00	10.00	30.00
701	Obv. 12, rev. M.........	8.00	10.00	15.00	20.00	50.00
702	Obv. 13, rev. M.........	2.00	4.00	6.00	10.00	30.00
703	Obv. 14, rev. M.........	150.00	200.00	250.00	300.00	

(Also see No. 691)

Twenty leaves in reverse wreath

Obv. 15 — 2 sham- rocks right, none left	Rev. N — small bow		Obv. 16 — 1 sham- rock right, 1 left	Rev. P — large bow

		V.G.	Fine	V.F.	E.F.	Unc.
704	Obv. 15, rev. N.........	2.00	4.00	6.00	10.00	30.00
705	Obv. 16, rev. P.........	3.00	5.00	8.00	12.00	35.00

II. Birmingham Issues

The sous numbered 706 through 712 were struck in Birmingham, England, by the firm that struck the early sous of the Bank of Montreal. Only two specimens are known of 712, which was not discovered until 1891. Some question of its authenticity exists, as the obverse in many ways resembles 691, which may have been struck in Belleville.

Thirty-two leaves in reverse wreath

Obv. 17 — 1 sham- rock right, none left	Obv. 18 — 2 sham- rocks left, none right	Obv. 19 — 3 sham- rocks left, none right

Obv. 20 —
English legend,
2 roses

Rev. R —
32 leaves

Breton No.	V.G.	Fine	V.F.	E.F.	Unc.
706 Obv. 17, rev. R	$7.00	$9.00	$12.00	$18.00	$40.00
707 Obv. 18, rev. R	2.00	4.00	6.00	10.00	30.00
708 Obv. 19, rev. R	2.50	5.00	8.00	12.00	35.00
709 Obv. 20, rev. R					
(obv. in English)	4.00	7.00	10.00	15.00	40.00

Forty-two leaves in reverse wreath

Obv. 21 — 2 large
shamrocks, 4 small

Obv. 22 — 1 sham-
rock right, 2 left

Rev. S — 42 leaves

710 Obv. 19, rev. S	4.00	7.00	10.00	15.00	40.00
711 Obv. 21, rev. S	3.00	5.00	8.00	12.00	35.00
712 Obv. 22, rev. S		2 known			

III. Miscellaneous Issues

Number 690 was unknown until 1870, and may have been struck in Boston, where most specimens were discovered. It is doubtful that it actually circulated, as most pieces are proofs. The origin of 691 is uncertain.

The remaining sous were all struck in Montreal. Number 674 was designed by Jean Marie Arnault, and was struck over various older tokens withdrawn from circulation. The dies and a few original specimens of 689 were found in Montreal in 1863. A small number of restrikes were struck in various metals after the dies had been fitted with a collar.

Obv. 23 —
1 shamrock right,
4 left

Rev. T — 16
small leaves

Breton No.	V.G.	Fine	V.F.	E.F.	Unc.
674 Obv. 23, rev. T (16 leaves), copper	$3.00	$5.00	$8.00	$15.00	
674a Obv. 23, rev. T, brass	2.00	4.00	6.00	10.00	

Obv. 24 — 4 sham-rocks right, 2 left / Rev. U — 17 leaves, with bow / Obv. 25 — sm. bou-quet, no shamrocks / Rev. V — small N's

684 Obv. 24, rev. U (17 leaves).	3.00	5.00	8.00	15.00	
689 Obv. 25, rev. V (18 leaves, no bow) original, struck without collar	30.00	50.00	75.00	100.00	
689a Obv. 25, rev. V, restrike, struck with collar			20.00	35.00	60.00

Obv. 26 — shamrocks with round leaves / Rev. W — 18 leaves, no bow / Obv. 27 — colon stops, no shamrocks / Rev. X — 18 leaves, with bow

690 Obv. 26, rev. W (18 leaves, no bow), the "Boston sou," struck as proof				100.00	175.00
691 Obv. 27, rev. X (18 leaves, with bow)	2.00	4.00	6.00	10.00	30.00

Later Bank Tokens 1838-39

Habitant Tokens

The Habitant tokens, so called because they show on the obverse a Canadian habitant in traditional winter costume, were released early in 1838. They were struck by Boulton & Watt. The Bank of Montreal, the Quebec Bank, the City Bank, and the Banque du Peuple participated in the issue, with the bank name appearing on the reverse ribbon. The Bank of Montreal is-sued 240,000 pennies and 480,000 halfpennies, and each of the others issued 120,000 pennies and 240,000 halfpennies.

231   235a

		V.G.	Fine	V.F.	E.F.	Unc.
231	City Bank Halfpenny	$1.50	$2.50	$4.00	$6.00	$25.00
232	Quebec Bank halfpenny	1.50	2.50	4.00	6.00	25.00
233	Banque du Peuple half-					
	penny	2.00	4.00	6.00	10.00	30.00
234	Bank of Montreal halfpenny	1.75	3.00	4.50	7.50	27.50
235	City Bank penny,					
	large ground	2.00	3.00	5.00	8.00	30.00
235a	Same, small ground	2.00	3.00	5.00	8.00	30.00
236	Quebec Bank penny,					
	large ground	2.50	3.50	6.00	9.00	35.00
236a	Same, small ground	2.50	3.50	6.00	9.00	35.00
237	Banque du Peuple,					
	large ground	4.00	6.00	9.00	12.50	40.00
237a	Same, small ground	3.00	4.50	7.50	10.00	35.00
238	Bank of Montreal,					
	large ground	2.50	3.50	6.00	9.00	35.00
238a	Same, small ground	2.50	3.50	6.00	9.00	35.00

Side View Tokens

The "Side View" tokens, so called because they show a corner view of the
Bank of Montreal building, were struck by Cotterill, Hill & Co. of Walsall,
England. In 1838 the coiners shipped 120,000 pennies and 240,000 halfpennies
to Montreal. The bank returned the coins because their workmanship was
far inferior to that of the Habitant tokens, and the copper was brassy. The
bank sent a Habitant penny as an example of the workmanship they required,
and asked for another shipment of equal size. In 1839 another 120,000 pennies
and 240,000 halfpennies arrived, but these were also returned on the ground
that they were even worse than the shipment of 1838.

Collectors today would disagree with the officials of the bank. The 1839
tokens are in better copper, and the fabric, though still not as good as that
of the Habitant coins, is less coarse than that of the 1838 coins.

All of the "Side View" coins were supposed to have been sent back and
melted down, but this was evidently not the case. Specimens of both dates
appear frequently in auction sales. Though neither issue is at all common,
pieces are available often enough to suggest that they are more expensive
than rare.

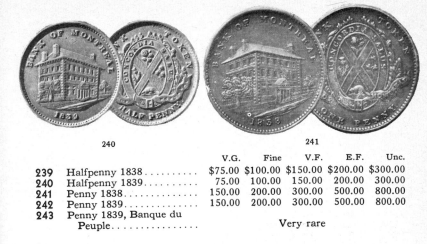

240   241

		V.G.	Fine	V.F.	E.F.	Unc.
239	Halfpenny 1838	$75.00	$100.00	$150.00	$200.00	$300.00
240	Halfpenny 1839	75.00	100.00	150.00	200.00	300.00
241	Penny 1838	150.00	200.00	300.00	500.00	800.00
242	Penny 1839	150.00	200.00	300.00	500.00	800.00
243	Penny 1839, Banque du Peuple			Very rare		

Transportation Tokens

Canada's earliest transportation tokens (244-255) appeared about 1807. They were issued to pay tolls across a series of bridges connecting the *Bout de l'Isle,* or east end of Montreal Island, to the mainland via Isle Bourdon. They were used only for a short time, for the bridges were all carried away by ice during the spring breakup. They were at once rebuilt, only to be demolished by ice again the next spring. They were not built again.

These pieces are very popular among collectors and are rare because the issue was rather small and used for such a short time. They were struck in Birmingham and bear two errors, the result of a carelessly written manuscript and the English engravers' ignorance of French. The inscriptions read ON and REPENTIGUY instead of OU and REPENTIGNY. Fakes were made of these tokens, but they were easily exposed because they were on thicker flans and bore lettering of a different style; also they have a five-pointed star instead of a six-rayed ornament under the word MONTREAL.

The Lachesnaye tokens are mostly clipped. This was done because the guardian of the Lachesnaye bridge could not read.

244

		V.G.	Fine	V.F.	E.F.
244	Lachesnaye, Caleche	50.00	75.00	100.00	125.00
245	Same, Charrette	50.00	75.00	100.00	125.00
246	Same, Cheval	50.00	75.00	100.00	125.00
247	Same, Personne	50.00	75.00	100.00	125.00

249   250

		V.G.	Fine	V.F.	E.F.
248	L'Isle de Montreal, Caleche	$50.00	$75.00	$100.00	$125.00
249	Same, Charrette	50.00	75.00	100.00	125.00
250	Same, Cheval	50.00	75.00	100.00	125.00
251	Same, Personne	50.00	75.00	100.00	125.00

252	Repentigny, Caleche	50.00	75.00	100.00	125.00
253	Same, Charrette	50.00	75.00	100.00	125.00
254	Same, Cheval	50.00	75.00	100.00	125.00
255	Same, Personne	50.00	75.00	100.00	125.00

The Lauzon tokens (256-258) paid the fare from Quebec to Levis on the ferry steamer "Lauzon." The ship was owned by John Goudie, who later sold it to J. McKenzie. Some of the tokens were counterstamped with McKenzie's initials. McKenzie later sold the ship to J. Thompson, who countermarked some of the tokens with his initials.

256   257

256	Lauzon 1821	100.00	150.00
257	Lauzon, counterstamped J. McK.	100.00	150.00
258	Lauzon, counterstamped J.T.	125.00	175.00

UPPER CANADA

In 1791 the Great Lakes region was detached from Quebec and organized as the colony of Upper Canada. It is now the province of Ontario. Very little coined money was in use before 1800. A few of the Wellington tokens trickled in from Lower Canada after 1814, and local tokens appeared about 1812.

The Copper Company Tokens

The tokens of the Copper Company of Upper Canada were struck by Boulton & Watt, probably as patterns for a copper coinage for Upper Canada which was not approved, but this cannot be definitely established. Since they were unknown in Canada before 1870, there is reason for the belief that they were made to gratify the desire of some English token collector of the eighteenth century to have something not found in other cabinets. Though Boulton & Watt did not stoop to catering to the cupidity of such status-seekers, the suspicion that this is the reason for the existence of this piece cannot be easily dispelled.

The original piece was designed by Ponthon, the obverse being adapted from that of a halfpenny token of Glasgow, Scotland. The so-called restrikes, purveyed in 1894 by an English coin dealer, are no such thing. They were struck from a different pair of dies, which may or may not have been made in 1794. Pieces struck from these dies show oval O's instead of round O's in COPPER COMPANY, and the date is more compact and in taller numerals. No. 261 is muled with the reverse of the pattern Myddleton token for Kentucky, and may have been struck between 1796 and 1800.

259   261

		Proof
259	Original 1794, copper.................................	$400.00
260	Later die, copper.....................................	200.00
260a	Later die, silver.....................................	400.00
261	Myddleton mule 1796, copper..........................	400.00

The Brock Tokens 1812-1816

The Brock tokens were struck in honor of Sir Isaac Brock, who was killed at the battle of Queenston Heights in 1812. They are light in weight, probably because Upper Canada was using "York Currency" at the time, the old standard of the state of New York. On this basis the Spanish dollar was rated at eight shillings. It was superseded by Halifax Currency in 1822. The Brock tokens became too plentiful after 1816, and fell into discredit. Note that 262 erroneously reads BROOK rather than BROCK.

		V.G.	Fine	V.F.	E.F.	Unc.
262	Sir Isaac Brock 1812......	$2.00	$3.00	$5.00	$8.00	$20.00

263	Monument 1816, round wreath...............	2.00	3.00	5.00	8.00	20.00
263a	Monument 1816, oval wreath...............	2.00	3.00	5.00	8.00	20.00

264	Ship 1816...............	12.00	15.00	25.00		

The Sloop Tokens 1815-1833

These tokens feature on their obverses a sloop, which was in those days the chief means of transportation on the Great Lakes. This obverse was the work of John Sheriff of Liverpool. The tokens are heavier, as Upper Canada by this time was using Halifax Currency. Most of them are antedated to evade the law against private tokens enacted in 1825. As this law became a dead letter, later issues bore the actual date of issue.

265

		V.G.	Fine	V.F.	E.F.	Unc.
265	Anvil 1820, bowsprit over A..............	$1.50	$2.00	$3.50	$6.00	$17.50
265a	Same, bowsprit over DA...	2.00	3.00	4.50	7.50	20.00

266   267

		V.G.	Fine	V.F.
266	UPPER CANADA on cask, 1821.................	12.00	15.00	25.00
267	JAMAICA on cask, 1821.....	100.00	150.00	175.00

		V.G.	Fine	V.F.	E.F.	Unc.
268	Plow 1823, bowsprit over A	2.25	3.50	5.00	8.50	20.00
268a	Same, bowsprit over DA...	2.25	3.50	5.00	8.50	20.00
269	Plow 1833..............	2.25	3.50	5.00	8.50	20.00

270a

		V.G.	Fine
270	Hunter 1815, bowsprit over A................	10.00	15.00
270a	Same, bowsprit over DA...	10.00	15.00

		V.G.	Fine	V.F.	E.F.	Unc.
271	Tools 1833, brass........	2.50	4.00	6.00	9.00	25.00

The Lesslie Tokens

These tokens were issued by a drug and book firm with shops in Toronto,
Dundas, and Kingston. The twopence was engraved by Thomas Wells Ingram
of Birmingham. It was struck before 1830, probably as early as 1822, the
date appearing on the coin. A specimen was found in the cornerstone during
the demolition of the old Court House of Hamilton, Ontario, which was built
in 1827. The first Lesslie halfpenny (272) was issued from 1824 to 1827; the
second (272a) was issued from 1828 to 1830.

		V.G.	Fine	V.F.	E.F.	Unc.
272	Lesslie Halfpenny.........	$2.50	$4.50	$7.00	$11.00	$25.00
272a	Same, comma after YORK ..	3.50	5.50	9.00	12.50	30.00

273	Twopence 1822..........	20.00	25.00	35.00	50.00	100.00

Miscellaneous Tokens

About 1830 two varieties of tokens inscribed, "No Labour No Bread" appeared in Toronto. On one variety the threshing floor is shown with a right
end almost perpendicular. On the other the right end is slanted considerably
upward to the right. These tokens were imported by Perrins Bros., a dry
goods firm, but were seized by the Customs Department and ordered to be
melted down. A large number of the coppers "fell to the floor," as it has
been so quaintly said, and so escaped the melting pot and entered circulation.
They were occasionally found in change as late as 1870.

		V.G.	Fine	V.F.	E.F.	Unc.
274	No Labour, vertical ground	$3.00	$5.00	$8.00	$12.00	$25.00
274a	Same, diagonal ground	3.00	5.00	8.00	12.00	25.00

In 1832 a halfpenny token (275) was issued of honest size and weight. It was struck by John Walker & Co. of Birmingham, who also struck the Thistle coinage of Nova Scotia. Like the Nova Scotia coinage of 1832, this coin shows the bust of George IV, even though it was then two years after his death. It is not yet known whether this piece is semi-regal or private.

275	George IV 1832	7.00	10.00	12.00	18.00	40.00

A few "blacksmith" tokens of Upper Canadian design are known. All are rare. One is an imitation of the sloop token 265. Another was created using the die of one of the "To Facilitate Trade" tokens (268-269) in the last stages of disintegration. The Riseing Sun Tavern piece was issued in Toronto. Like the similar pieces of Lower Canada, these were first cataloged by Howland Wood.

	Wood No.		Fair	Good	V.G.
276	31	Sloop in wreath.	30.00	50.00	75.00

	Wood No.		Fair	Good	V.G.
277	45	To Facilitate Trade................	$30.00	$50.00	$75.00

278	24	Riseing Sun Tavern................	20.00	40.00	60.00

THE PROVINCE OF CANADA

Bank of Montreal Tokens 1842-1845

In 1841 Upper and Lower Canada were reunited to form the colony or province of Canada. The Bank of Montreal was given the right to coin copper, and it issued 240,000 pennies and 480,000 halfpennies in 1842. A further issue of 1,440,000 halfpennies was released in 1844. The coins were struck by Boulton & Watt. A halfpenny die was prepared in 1845, and two coins struck, but the bank did not issue any coins dated 1845.

The 1837 mule (283) dated 1837 is probably a concoction by W. J. Taylor. Taylor acquired all the Boulton & Watt dies when that firm went into liquidation. Among these dies were those of the Bank of Montreal coinage of 1842-1844, the Habitant coinage of 1837, and the 1843 coinage of New Brunswick. Some time afterward Taylor began to restrike from the dies, creating numerous mules. It is known that the dies used to produce 283 were not used for any variety of the 1837 or 1842 coinages. Also, the mule is lighter in weight than the pennies of either 1837 or 1842. The coin was unknown in Canada before 1870, and is not known in worn condition.

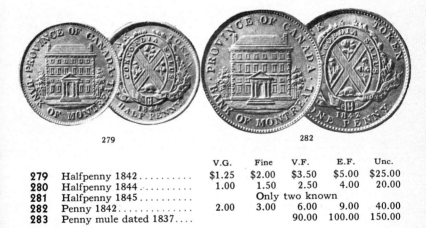

279   282

		V.G.	Fine	V.F.	E.F.	Unc.
279	Halfpenny 1842	$1.25	$2.00	$3.50	$5.00	$25.00
280	Halfpenny 1844	1.00	1.50	2.50	4.00	20.00
281	Halfpenny 1845		Only two known			
282	Penny 1842	2.00	3.00	6.00	9.00	40.00
283	Penny mule dated 1837....			90.00	100.00	150.00

Quebec Bank Tokens 1852

In 1852 the Quebec Bank was allowed to issue pennies and halfpennies because of a serious shortage of copper in Quebec. The Bank of Upper Canada coinage was supposed to be enough for the whole province, but the first two issues of this bank were not delivered until 1853, and the Quebec Bank was desperate. With government sanction the bank issued 240,000 pennies and 480,000 halfpennies in 1852. A request for permission to issue more was turned down on the grounds that a change to decimal currency was under contemplation, which event took place in 1858. The Quebec Bank pieces were struck by Ralph Heaton & Sons, and are among the most attractive Canadian colonial issues.

		V.G.	Fine	V.F.	E.F.	Unc.
284	Quebec Bank halfpenny 1852	$1.50	$2.50	$4.00	$6.00	$30.00
285	Quebec Bank penny 1852	2.00	3.00	6.00	9.00	35.00

Bank of Upper Canada Tokens 1850-1857

The Bank of Upper Canada received the right to issue copper in 1850, after the capital was transferred to Toronto from Montreal. An order was placed for 750,000 pennies and 1,500,000 halfpennies in 1850. The coins were struck by Ralph Heaton & Sons, but owing to pressure on their facilities, the firm could not deliver the coins until 1852. In 1852 the bank ordered another 750,000 pennies and 1,500,000 halfpennies from Heaton, which were delivered in 1853. A third issue of 750,000 pennies and 1,500,000 halfpennies took place in 1854. The final coinage was in 1857, when 1,500,000 pennies and 3,000,000 halfpennies were ordered. About half this issue was put into circulation, the remainder being unissued because of the adoption of decimal currency in 1858. Because of their design, the pieces often are called the "St. George" tokens.

The penny of 1852 with a narrow 2 in the date always comes with an upset reverse. Those with a small or wide 2 always have a straight reverse. The large 2 variety may have either a straight or upset reverse.

The Bank of Upper Canada was liquidated in 1867. Among its assets were eleven tons of copper coins lying in all their pristine redness in the vaults. These were sold as bullion and all were to have been melted down. However, the availability of uncirculated specimens, particularly of the 1857 issue, suggests that some, at least, "fell to the floor" rather than into the melting pot.

The initials on the ground at the right of the obverse are the initials of Rowe, Kentish & Co., the agents through whom the government placed the orders for the coinage. A look through a strong glass will definitely show them to be R K & CO. and not the initials of Ralph Heaton & Sons.

		V.G.	Fine	V.F.	E.F.	Unc.
286	Halfpenny 1850..........	$1.00	$1.50	$2.00	$4.00	$10.00
287	Halfpenny 1852..........	1.00	1.50	2.00	4.00	10.00
288	Halfpenny 1854, plain 4...	1.00	1.50	2.00	4.00	10.00
288a	Same, crosslet 4.........	15.00	20.00	25.00	35.00	60.00
289	Halfpenny 1857.........	1.00	1.50	2.00	4.00	10.00

290	Penny 1850..............	1.50	2.00	2.50	5.00	15.00
290a	Same, dot between					
	cornucopiae tips........	3.00	5.00	7.50	10.00	25.00

| 291 | 291a | 292a |

291	Penny 1852, narrow 2.....	1.50	2.00	2.50	5.00	15.00
291a	Same, large 2............	2.00	3.00	4.00	7.00	20.00
291b	Same, small 2............	3.00	5.00	7.50	10.00	25.00
291c	Same, wide 2............	3.00	5.00	8.00	12.50	30.00
292	Penny 1854, plain 4.......	1.50	2.00	2.50	5.00	15.00
292a	Same, crosslet 4.........	4.00	6.00	8.00	12.50	30.00
293	Penny 1857..............	1.50	2.00	2.50	5.00	15.00

Miscellaneous Pieces

The year 1852 saw the issue of the first trade token in Canada. In that year the Hunterstown Lumber Company issued a brass token valid only in Hunterstown, Quebec. It was redeemable in goods at the company store, and was valued at a halfpenny. It did not enjoy circulation throughout the province, and was not redeemable in money. The piece is rare.

	V.G.	Fine	V.F.	E.F.	Unc.
294 Hunterstown token 1852...	$125.00	$150.00	$175.00	$225.00	$300.00

The Montreal & Lachine Railroad was opened in 1847. Third class fares were paid by means of a copper token perforated in the center so that they could be strung on a wire when collected. The tokens were in use until 1862.

295 Montreal & Lachine Railroad..............	30.00	45.00	60.00	75.00	100.00

Encased postage stamps were invented in the United States when nearly all coins vanished in the early years of the Civil War. There was never any need for them in Canada, but one of the partners of the firm of Weir & Larminie of Montreal had a few made after seeing examples on a visit to New York. They are very rare, especially those containing Canadian postage stamps.

296a

		Fair	Good	V.G.
296	Encased U.S. 1¢ stamp.................	200.00	250.00	300.00
296a	Encased U.S. 3¢, 5¢, or 10¢ stamp........	175.00	200.00	250.00
296b	Encased Canadian stamp................	300.00	400.00	500.00

What was loosely termed "the Northwest" in colonial times included all of British North America north and west of colonial Canada to the Pacific coast and the Arctic Archipelago. This vast region was the preserve of the Hudson's Bay Company. No settlement took place anywhere in this region before Lord Selkirk opened up the valley of the Red River, later to become the province of Manitoba. Beyond this area the only permanent establishments were the trading posts of the Hudson's Bay Company and its rival, the Northwest Company. After years of bitter strife the two companies merged in 1821.

On the west coast, Vancouver Island was detached from the Company and set up as a Crown Colony. The British Columbia mainland was separated in 1858 as a second Crown Colony. In 1866 these two colonies united, and the united colony entered the Dominion of Canada in 1871. The remainder of the territory of the Hudson's Bay Company was acquired by the Dominion of Canada in 1869.

Northwest Company Token 1820

The Northwest Company token was struck in Birmingham in 1820. It is not known by whom, but its style suggests that it may have been struck by John Walker & Co., who struck the Nova Scotia coinage of 1823-1843. All known specimens of this piece were found in the lower valley of the Columbia River in Oregon, which is now in the United States. For this reason it is considered an American piece. It is also thought of as Canadian because it was issued by a Canadian firm, although no specimens have yet been found in Canada.

		Fair	Good	V.G.	Fine
297	Northwest Company, copper.......	$100.00	$150.00	$225.00	$350.00
297a	Same, brass....................	150.00	225.00	300.00	450.00

Hudson's Bay Company Tokens

The brass tokens of the Hudson's Bay Company were issued around 1854. At the top of the reverse is the Company's **HB** monogram, below which are the initials **EM** for the East Main district, south and east of Hudson Bay. The tokens have been found in northern Quebec and Ontario, and as far

west as Manitoba. They are erroneously valued in "new beaver." The unit
of the fur trade was the "made beaver," which is an adult beaver skin in
prime condition. It was never cut up, and so the Company thought that
tokens would be the ideal way in which to express fractions of the made
beaver. The Indians, however, preferred to trust the Company accounts
rather than take the tokens, which were easily lost. For this reason the pieces
never circulated in large quantities. When it was decided to redeem them,
the tokens were punched on the reverse at the top to show that they had
been redeemed and cancelled. The number of unpunched pieces available now
suggests that they were not all presented to be redeemed, or that not all
company offices punched them as they were redeemed.

		V.G.	Fine	V.F.	E.F.	Unc.
298	⅛ made beaver.........	$20.00	$25.00	$30.00	$40.00	$60.00
299	¼ made beaver.........	20.00	25.00	30.00	40.00	60.00
300	½ made beaver.........	20.00	25.00	30.00	40.00	60.00
301	1 made beaver..........	20.00	25.00	30.00	40.00	60.00

13

MODERN PAPER MONEY

BANK OF CANADA ISSUES 1935 TO DATE

Many photos in this section courtesy Walter D. Allan.

The Bank of Canada was created by the Central Bank Act of 1934. Under that Act the Bank was given sole responsibility for the issuance of Canadian paper money, though chartered banks continued to issue their own notes into the early 1940's (the last being the Royal Bank of Canada in 1943). By 1950 these banks had transferred the responsibility for redemption of

Two examples of chartered bank notes, Barclays Bank (Canada) and Bank of Toronto

their banknotes to the Bank of Canada, thus guaranteeing any of their notes yet outstanding.

FIRST ISSUE 1935

The 1935 issue was the first in the reduced modern size of 6 x 2⅞ inches. The decision to reduce the size of circulating banknotes had been reached in 1932 but not implemented until this first Bank of Canada issue.

On March 11, 1935, the initial release took place; portraits on the notes were in most cases members of the Royal Family. The 1935 issue was unique

$1 1935, English and French issues

in that it consisted of not one but two separate and complete emissions, the first in English and the second in French. Except for language and serial number prefix, the design and other details are identical.

The $25 Commemorative Issue

On May 6, 1935, a $25 commemorative note was released in limited quantities. It, too, was made in the English and French versions, the latter being much the scarcer of the two. The occasion was the 25th anniversary of the

[151]

$25 Commemorative, face and back, French issue

$25 Commemorative, English issue

accession of King George V and Queen Mary. The notes are dated "Ottawa, May 6th 1935." At the top are the dates 1910-1935.

General Specifications

All notes were printed on planchette paper (planchettes are tiny colored discs embedded in the paper during its manufacture as an anti-counterfeiting device) by two firms, the Canadian Bank Note Company Ltd. and the British American Bank Note Company Ltd., both of Ottawa. Each note bears facsimile signatures of J. A. C. Osborne as Deputy Governor and G. F. Towers as Governor (of the Bank). All except the $25 bear the designation "Ottawa, issue of 1935" (in English or French).

Portraits, Back Designs, and Colors for the 1935 Issue

Denom.	Portrait	Back Design	Basic Color
$1	King George V	Allegorical figure of Agriculture	Green
$2	Queen Mary	Mercury with implements of transportation	Blue
$5	Prince of Wales, later Edward VIII, now Duke of Windsor	Allegorical figure of Power	Orange

$2 1935, French issue $5 1935, French issue

$10......Princess Royal

$20......Princess Elizabeth, now Elizabeth II

$25......King George V and Queen Mary

$50......Duke of York, later George VI

Allegorical figure of Harvest................Purple

Worker showing produce to Agriculture...........Rose pink

Windsor Castle..........Royal purple

Allegorical figure of Invention with radio.....Brown

$10 1935, English issue

$10 1935, French issue

$20 1935, French issue

$50 1935, English issue

$1000 1935, face side of English issue

$1000 1935, back of French issue

$100.....Duke of Gloucester

$500.....Sir John A. MacDonald, first Prime Minister of the Dominion in 1867

$1000....Sir Wilfrid Laurier, Prime Minister 1896-1911

Allegorical scene of Shipping with industry.......Dark brown

Allegorical scene showing Produce........Tan

Allegorical figure of Security................Olive green

1935 ENGLISH ISSUE

Denom.	V.G.	Fine	V.F.	E.F.	New
$1....	$2.00	$2.50	$3.50	$4.25	$12.00
$2....	2.75	3.00	3.75	4.50	14.00
$5....	7.50	8.00	10.00	15.00	45.00
$10...	10.50	11.00	12.00	14.00	30.00
$20...	24.00	26.00	32.00	38.00	65.00
$25...	80.00	120.00	175.00	240.00	325.00
$50...	52.00	55.00	60.00	70.00	100.00
$100..	102.00	105.00	112.00	120.00	150.00
$500..	510.00	520.00	535.00	550.00	650.00
$1000.		1,005	1,010	1,025	1,100

1935 FRENCH ISSUE

V.G.	Fine	V.F.	E.F.	New
$2.25	$2.75	$3.75	$5.00	$15.00
3.00	3.50	4.50	7.00	24.00
8.00	8.50	10.50	20.00	60.00
11.00	12.00	14.00	17.00	38.00
25.00	28.00	35.00	42.00	75.00
100.00	145.00	185.00	260.00	525.00
55.00	58.00	65.00	75.00	125.00
105.00	110.00	115.00	125.00	160.00
515.00	525.00	540.00	555.00	675.00
	1,005	1,010	1,025	1,150

All the English issues have the letter **A** in front of the serial number (except the $1 which also has a letter **B,** much scarcer than the **A** issue). All the French issues have the letter **F** in front of the serial number.

Low serial numbers in both English and French issues command a premium of 25% to 100% above the listed valuations.

SECOND ISSUE 1937

The next issue of Bank of Canada notes appeared in 1937 under George VI. A number of major changes took place from the previous issue. All notes except two portrayed George VI, and the issue consisted of bi-lingual notes in every instance as the cost of preparing separate issues had been too high.

Typical face side — George VI   Typical allegorical back

The $100 showed Sir John A. MacDonald and the $1000 portrayed Sir Wilfrid Laurier. The $500 denomination was discontinued.

Back Designs and Colors

All back designs of the 1937 notes were holdovers from the 1935 issue, though they did not necessarily appear on the same denominations as previously.

Denom.	Back Design	Basic Color	Denom.	Back Design	Basic Color
$1.....	Same as 1935....	Green	$20....	As $500 1935....	Olive green
$2.....	As $10 1935.....	Dull red	$50....	Same as 1935....	Orange
$5.....	Same as 1935....	Blue	$100...	Same as 1935....	Brown
$10....	As $2 1935......	Purple	$1000..	Same as 1935....	Pink

Date and Signature Combinations

All notes of the 1937 issue bear the date January 2, 1937. There are three signature combinations on these notes, as follows:

J. A. C. Osborne and G. F. Towers — D. Gordon and G. F. Towers
J. E. Coyne and G. F. Towers

Denom.	Signatures	V.G.	Fine	V.F.	E.F.	New
$1	Osborne-Towers....	$1.50	$2.00	$3.50	$7.00	$16.00
	Gordon-Towers....	1.10	1.25	1.50	2.00	7.00
	Coyne-Towers.....	1.10	1.20	1.45	1.80	5.00
$2	Osborne-Towers....	2.50	3.00	4.50	8.00	20.00
	Gordon-Towers....	2.25	2.40	2.50	3.00	8.00
	Coyne-Towers.....	2.15	2.25	2.35	2.75	6.00
$5	Osborne-Towers....	8.00	10.00	15.00	20.00	35.00
	Gordon-Towers....	5.25	5.75	7.00	9.00	15.00
	Coyne-Towers.....	5.25	5.75	6.50	7.50	12.00
$10	Osborne-Towers....	11.50	12.50	14.00	16.00	25.00
	Gordon-Towers...............			10.25	10.50	18.00
	Coyne-Towers..................			10.25	14.00	
$20	Osborne-Towers....	21.00	21.50	23.00	25.00	35.00
	Gordon-Towers..................				20.50	26.00
	Coyne-Towers..................					23.00
$50	Osborne-Towers..................					75.00
	Gordon-Towers..................					65.00
	Coyne-Towers..................					55.00
$100	Osborne-Towers..................					125.00
	Gordon-Towers..................					115.00
	Coyne-Towers..................					110.00
$1000	Valuation varies from $1,050 to $1,200 in New condition.					

THIRD ISSUE 1954

Upon the death of George VI in 1952, a new issue of Canadian currency was prepared for the incoming ruler, Elizabeth II. Her initial issue appeared in

Typical face side with portrait   Typical back with Canadian scene

1954, and once again a number of departures from previous issues were incorporated. The Queen appeared on all denominations, on the face side and at the right. Back designs were drastically changed from allegorical vignettes to typical scenes of Canada, as follows:

Denom.	Back Design	Denom.	Back Design
$1	Western prairie and sky	$20	Laurentian Hills in winter
$2	Country valley in Central Canada	$50	Atlantic seashore
		$100	Mountain, valley and lake
$5	Northern stream and forest	$1000	Village, lake and hills
$10	Rocky Mountain peak		

Basic colors for all denominations were carried over from the previous issue.

The "Devil in the Hair" Variety

Shortly after the 1954 issue appeared, the "devil" was discovered in the Queen's hair. Certain unshaded portions of her hair created the illusion of

"Devil in the Hair" variety   Modified coiffure

an ugly face behind the ear. All denominations were issued using the "devil" plates, but before too long new plates with a re-done coiffure eliminated the apparition.

Date and Signature Combinations

All notes of the first issue of Elizabeth carry the designation "Ottawa, 1954." There are three signature combinations in this issue:

    J. E. Coyne and G. F. Towers (all come with the "devil")
    J. R. Beattie and J. E. Coyne (with and without the "devil")
    J. R. Beattie and L. Rasminsky

The $1 Centennial Commemorative of 1967

As part of the celebration of the centennial of Canadian confederation, a special $1 note was made and issued in two varieties. The first of these carried

$1 1967 Commemorative, face and back

dates 1867 1967 instead of serial numbers and the second bore regular serial numbers. Only the latter was issued to circulation, the former being available only from the Bank of Canada as a collector's item. Both varieties proved very popular, but the majority of those saved were the 1867 1967 collector's issue. The design was a departure from the regular note, especially on the back where a vignette of the old Parliament Buildings created a very attractive effect.

Denom.	Signatures	V.F.	E.F.	New
$1	Coyne-Towers	$1.25	$1.75	$4.00
	Beattie-Coyne w/devil	1.15	1.35	3.00
	Beattie-Coyne plain		1.15	2.00
	Beattie-Rasminsky			1.25
	1967 Commemorative, dates 1867 1967			1.25
	1967 as above, with regular serial numbers			2.00
	1967 as above with asterisk in front of serial number (replacement note)			2.50
$2	Coyne-Towers	2.25	2.50	5.00
	Beattie-Coyne w/devil	2.10	2.25	4.00
	Beattie-Coyne plain			3.00
	Beattie-Rasminsky			2.25
$5	Coyne-Towers		5.25	8.00
	Beattie-Coyne w/devil		5.25	7.00
	Beattie-Coyne plain			6.00
	Beattie-Rasminsky			5.25
$10	Coyne-Towers		10.50	15.00
	Beattie-Coyne w/devil			13.00
	Beattie-Coyne plain			11.00
	Beattie-Rasminsky			10.50
$20	Coyne-Towers		21.50	30.00
	Beattie-Coyne w/devil		21.00	26.00
	Beattie-Coyne plain			24.00
	Beattie-Rasminsky			21.00
$50	Coyne-Towers			plus 20% over face
$100	Beattie-Coyne w/devil			plus 10% over face
$1000	Beattie-Coyne plain			plus 5% over face
	Beattie-Rasminsky			face value only

Asterisk or Replacement Notes

With the 1954 issue Canada began the issuance of replacement notes to substitute for those damaged during production. Such notes were marked

Asterisk note

with an asterisk preceding the letters in the serial number. Previous to this issue, no indications were placed on notes used for replacement of defective specimens. Asterisk notes enjoy great popularity and are thus cataloged sep-

arately. Some are very scarce, and nothing over the $20 denomination has
been verified with the asterisk.

Denom.	Signatures	V.G.	New
$1	Coyne-Towers*	$25.00	$125.00
	Beattie-Coyne w/devil*	10.00	50.00
	Beattie-Coyne plain*		2.50
	Beattie-Rasminsky*		1.25
$2	Coyne-Towers*	35.00	150.00
	Beattie-Coyne w/devil*	10.00	60.00
	Beattie-Coyne plain*		3.00
	Beattie-Rasminsky*		2.35
$5	Coyne-Towers*	50.00	200.00
	Beattie-Coyne w/devil*	15.00	65.00
	Beattie-Coyne plain*		8.00
	Beattie-Rasminsky*		5.50
$10	Coyne-Towers*	35.00	150.00
	Beattie-Coyne w/devil*	20.00	65.00
	Beattie-Coyne plain*		15.00
	Beattie-Rasminsky*		10.75
$20	Coyne-Towers*	50.00	200.00
	Beattie-Coyne w/devil*	30.00	75.00
	Beattie-Coyne plain*		25.00
	Beattie-Rasminsky*		21.50

FOURTH ISSUE 1969

A completely new issue of banknotes is now in the planning stage. Main
features of the new notes will be their security devices which include a more
complicated engraving process and a greater usage of color variety. The first
note of the new series is the $20 which was released in June of 1970; it carries
the designation "Ottawa 1969." Both regular and asterisk notes are verified.
Signatures of Beattie and Rasminsky have been retained from the previous
issue.

The new $20 is very striking, especially on the face side where a rainbow
effect is created by the intermingling of colors. The coat of arms is in full
color at the left, and serial numbers are red at left and blue at right. The
Queen's portrait, newly designed, appears at the right. On the back is a scene

from the Canadian Rocky Mountains. Predominant color is olive green.

Other denominations in the proposed new series will carry portraits as
follows:

Denom.	Portrait	Denom.	Portrait
$1	Queen Elizabeth II	$20	See above description
$2	Queen Elizabeth II	$50	William L. MacKenzie King
$5	Sir Wilfrid Laurier	$100	Sir Robert Borden
$10	Sir John A. MacDonald		

BIBLIOGRAPHY

GENERAL

Breton, P.N. *Illustrated History of Coins and Tokens Relating to Canada.* Montreal, 1894 (reprinted 1963).

Davis, W. J. *The Nineteenth Century Token Coinage.* 1904 (reprinted 1969).

Leroux, Joseph. *The Canadian Coin Cabinet.* Montreal, 1888.

NEW FRANCE

Blanchet, Adrien, and Dieudonne, Adolphe. *Manuel de numismatique française.* 4 vols., Paris, 1912-1936.

Breen, Walter. "The Billon Sous Marqués of Canada." *Whitman Numismatic Journal,* August-October 1965.

Ciani, Louis. *Les monnaies royales françaises de Hugues Capet à Louis XVI.* Paris, 1926 (reprinted 1969).

Mazard, Jean. *Histoire monétaire et numismatique des colonies et de l'Union Française 1670-1952.* Paris, 1953.

Willey, Robert C. "The Coinages of New France." *Whitman Numismatic Journal,* July 1965.

————— "The Numismatics of the French Regime Re-examined." *Transactions of the Canadian Numismatic Research Society,* October 1969, April 1970.

Zay, E. *Histoire monétaire des colonies françaises.* Paris, 1892 (reprinted 1969).

ANONYMOUS PIECES

Courteau, Eugene G. "The Non-Local Tokens of Canada." *The Numismatist,* May 1924.

NEWFOUNDLAND

Courteau, Eugene G. "The Coins and Tokens of Newfoundland." *The Numismatist,* February 1930.

PRINCE EDWARD ISLAND

Bowman, Fred, and Stewart, H. R. "The Prince Edward Island and Other Holey Dollars." *The Canadian Numismatic Journal,* April 1960.

Byrne, Ray. "The World's 'Holey' Dollars." *The Numismatist,* March 1970.

Courteau, Eugene G. "The Coins and Tokens of Prince Edward Island." *The Numismatist,* November 1922.

Lees, W. A. D. "The Ships, Colonies & Commerce Tokens." *The Numismatist,* January 1917.

Pridmore, F. "The Holey Dollar and Plug of Prince Edward Island." *Spink & Son's Numismatic Circular,* November, December 1960.

Reid, R. L. "The Holey Dollar of Prince Edward Island." *The Numismatist,* February 1929.

NOVA SCOTIA

Courteau, Eugene G. *The Coins and Tokens of Nova Scotia.* St-Jacques, 1910.

McLachlan, Robert Wallace. *Annals of the Nova Scotia Coinage.* Montreal, 1892.

NEW BRUNSWICK

Courteau, Eugene G. "The Coins and Tokens of New Brunswick." *The Numismatist,* August 1923.

LOWER CANADA

Bowman, Fred. "The Bouquet Sou Tokens of Canada." *The Numismatist,* July-November 1955; reprinted in *The Canadian Numismatic Journal,* January, February 1960.

Courteau, Eugene G. "The Canadian 1820 Bust and Harp Tokens." *The Numismatist,* May, June 1907.

————— *The Canadian Bouquet-Sous.* St-Jacques, 1908.

————— "The Wellington Tokens Relating to Canada." *Proceedings of the American Numismatic Society,* 1914.

————— *The Copper Tokens of the Bank of Montreal.* St-Jacques, 1919.

————— "The Non-Local Tokens of Canada." *The Numismatist,* May 1924.

————— *The Habitant Tokens of Lower Canada.* St-Jacques, 1927.

————— "The Canadian Bust and Commerce Tokens." *The Numismatist,* February 1934.

McLachlan, R. W. "The Copper Coinage of the Canadian Banks." Royal Society of Canada Transactions, 1903.

Willey, Robert C. "Num Illos Vis Capere?" *Whitman Numismatic Journal,* April 1966.

Wood, Howland. "The Canadian Blacksmith Coppers." *The Numismatist,* April 1910.

UPPER CANADA

McLachlan, R. W. "The Copper Tokens of Upper Canada." *The American Journal of Numismatics,* 1915.

Willey, Robert C. "The Coinage of Upper Canada." *Whitman Numismatic Journal,* September, October 1966.

PROVINCE OF CANADA

Courteau, Eugene G. *The Copper Tokens of the Bank of Montreal.* St-Jacques, 1919.

——————— *The St. George Copper Tokens of the Bank of Upper Canada.* St-Jacques, 1934.

McLachlan, R. W. "The Copper Currency of the Canadian Banks." Royal Society of Canada Transactions, 1903.

MODERN DECIMAL ISSUES

Bowman, F. "The Decimal Coinage of Canada and Newfoundland." *The Numismatist,* March 1947.

Cashin, F. Personal communication with the authors.

New Netherlands Coin Co., Inc. *58th Catalogue.* New York, September 22-23, 1964.

——————— *59th Catalogue.* New York, June 13-15, 1967.

Peck, C. Wilson. *English Copper, Tin and Bronze Coins in the British Museum.* London, 1960.

Royal Canadian Mint. *Report of the Master of the Royal Canadian Mint.* Annual vols., Ottawa, 1935 to date.

——————— Personal communications with the authors.

Royal Mint. *Annual Report of the Deputy Master and Comptroller.* Annual vols., London, 1870 to date.

——————— *Catalogue of the Coins, Tokens, Medals, Dies and Seals in the Museum of the Royal Mint.* 2 vols., London, 1906-1910.

——————— Personal communications with the authors.